Night Train
to Turkistan

NIGHT
TRAIN
TO
TURKISTAN

Modern Adventures
Along China's
Ancient Silk Road

STUART STEVENS

THE ATLANTIC MONTHLY PRESS
NEW YORK

The author would like to thank Jeremy P. Tarcher, Inc., for permission to
quote from *News From Tartary* by Peter Fleming, copyright © 1936 by Peter
Fleming.

Published simultaneously in Canada
Printed in the United States of America

Library of Congress Cataloging-in-Publication Data

Stevens, Stuart.
    Night train to Turkistan : modern adventures along China's ancient silk
road / Stuart Stevens.
    ISBN 0-87113-190-0
    1. China—Description and travel—1976– 2. Silk Road—Description
and travel. 3. Stevens, Stuart—Journeys—China. 4. Stevens,
Stuart—Journeys—Silk Road. I. Title.
DS712.S74 1988
915.1'0458—dc19   87-30019

Design by Laura Hammond Hough

Atlantic Monthly Press
841 Broadway
New York, NY 10003

99 00 01 02 15 14 13 12 11 10 9 8

To my family,
intrepid travelers in their own way,
and C.A.N.

NIGHT TRAIN
TO
TURKISTAN

0   MILES   400

0   KM   400

U.S.S.R

Urumqi

Turpan

TURFAN DEPRESSION

Korla

Aksu

CHINESE TURKISTAN

TAKLA MAKAN

Fleming's Route

Kashgar

AFGHAN

PAKISTAN

TIBET

Llasa

INDIA

The use of traveling is to regulate imagination with reality and, instead of thinking how things might be, to see them as they are.

Dr. Samuel Johnson

Night Train
to Turkistan

Prologue

Everyone talked about the snow. It had been coming
down for four days straight; such extremes shocked
Geneva, a city boastful of its moderation.

I had seen a lot of snow. Kashgar was covered and
more fell in Beijing the morning I boarded the Trans-
Siberian. Mongolia and Siberia were white, and Moscow
had been a blizzard.

But I welcome the Geneva storm. It quieted the city
and made it easier for me to concentrate on eating and
sleeping. In brief bouts of wakefulness, I roamed out from
my hotel in the old city to devour huge meals. I ate everything. Except lamb. It would take a while for that taste to
come back.

"There's still a pile of snow out front on the walk, but
I think you can make it through. I'm on the fifth floor, just
come on up." Her voice was firm, tinged with a trace of
laughter. She didn't sound eighty-three.

Her apartment wasn't far, a half-hour on foot, just
beyond the boundaries of the old city. Walking over, I
reveled in the familiarity of the Swiss scene—the yellow
PTT buses, the policemen in their pillbox hats, the army
of snow shovelers in their bright orange jump suits. I had
once lived in this country and though it wasn't really
home, it now felt predictable and comfortable and just
what I needed. Even the way pedestrians and drivers rig-

idly obeyed traffic signs, a little thing that used to drive me crazy, was now pleasantly reassuring.

The elevator in her building was an old-fashioned iron cage rising through the center of a marble staircase. "Mlle. Ella Maillart," read the card on the oak door.

"I've come all the way around the world just to see you," I'd explained on the phone and we'd laughed, if only because it was true. Now I was nervous. I knew why I wanted to see her but I wasn't sure what I would say.

She held herself canted slightly to the left, a small woman with seeping gray hair and bright eyes. Her left hand came out for a firm shake; her right was bandaged in thick guaze.

"I've been looking at some pictures," she said, pulling me into the apartment. It was two sunny rooms crowded with antiques. "Why didn't you plan better?" she asked.

"Plan better?"

"Here look . . ." She pointed to a worn map of China. A black line snaked from Beijing to Kashgar.

"Was this the map you carried?" I asked.

She laughed. "Of course not! This is a Communist map!"

I looked closer. All of the lettering was in French. Kashgar was located in the "Region Autonome Ouigoure du Xin Jiang." This struck me as funny.

"But tell me," she asked, "why did you not penetrate to the Takla Makan?" Her finger traced the oblong brown section of the map outlining the great desert of Western China.

"But we did. Here, I'll show you." We pulled up chairs, sat down at the large coffee table, and quickly got lost somewhere out in Chinese Turkistan. Mostly she talked and I listened. It grew very warm in the bright, small room. I was still in the habit of wearing four or five

4

layers of clothes. The idea of heated rooms was an adjustment I hadn't made.

We talked about places like Golmud and Xinning, Hotan and Kashgar. Once they had just been odd-sounding names in her book and on a map. But now they meant something to me, had become a part of my past as well.

After a couple of hours, she stood suddenly and announced, "I've talked too much. Let's go to lunch in a little place I like around the corner and I can hear more about what you saw and how it has changed in fifty years.

"But tell me again, why is it you wanted to do such a thing?"

Chapter One

From the beginning it was a silly idea, without the slightest utilitarian purpose or merit. This, of course, I liked.

The scheme was to retrace Peter Fleming and Ella Maillart's 1935 journey from Beijing to India via Kashgar. Their's was a preposterous trip made by the most unlikely of companions. A young English aristocrat from a family of notable eccentrics teamed with a decidedly down-to-earth Swiss woman who was a member of the Swiss national sailing team. That they happened to be traveling through the area farthest from any ocean on the face of the earth seemed in complete keeping with the tone of the venture. Fleming was in a rush to get back to England in time for the grouse-hunting season; Maillart could have, as she put it, "spent her life learning more about Chinese Turkistan and its people." To Fleming—who once dissuaded a friend from beating up an incompetent native guide in Brazil by pointing out how rude it was to hit your butler—a life in Turkistan would have been a sentence.

Both wrote books about the adventure; Peter Fleming's 1936 *News From Tartary* was a trans-Atlantic hit, confirming his position as a literary leader of a post-World War I generation gone travel mad. Ella Maillart—or Kini, as everyone called her—titled her book *Forbidden Journey*. It made her a celebrity, one of the few women to participate in the travel-writing craze.

The big question, naturally, was whether the two were lovers. That and what sort of gun Fleming should have taken with him:

> Sirs:
>
> It is difficult to comprehend the foolishness of setting across Asia on foot armed only, as we are to believe Mr. Peter Fleming was, with a defective .44 and a .22 sporting rifle. The "Times" would have done well to present their Special Correspondent with a proper .256 Mannlicher. Had Mr. Fleming been called upon, as he had reason to believe he might, to shoot himself out of a tight corner, his childish .22, which he refers to lovingly as a "rook" rifle, would hardly have served his purposes well.
>
> Respectfully,
> Mr. T.B. Money-Coutts

> Sirs:
>
> I wonder how those who look on a .22 as a childish toy would like to make a target of the plump part of their own back view at 100 yards —or even 150—for a good .22 cartridge.
>
> Lieutenant-Colonel G.A. Anson

This was all very serious stuff for *Times'* readers; the topic dominated the avidly read letters section for months after Fleming's account of the trip appeared in the spring of 1936. The other question, the sexual one, regrettably never made it into print. (Though it's true that when King Edward shocked the world in the summer of '36 by slipping off to the Mediterranean on a pleasure yacht with Mrs. Simpson, a trip around which rumors of nude sunbathing swirled, the press duly noted that everyone on board was reading *News From Tartary*.)

That Fleming and Maillart were traveling at all together was an acute embarrassment to both. His last book had been titled *One's Company;* her's was *Turkistan Solo.* Each revered the idea of "going it alone" and had substantial literary capital invested in their images of lone voyagers. In *One's Company* Fleming had even gone to the trouble to give an overelaborate description of the joys of a party of one:

> It is easy enough for one man to adapt himself to living under strange and constantly changing conditions. It is much harder for two. Leave A or B alone in a distant country, and each will evolve a congenial *modus vivendi.* Throw them together, and the comforts of companionship are as likely as not offset by the strain of reconciling their divergent methods. A likes to start early and halt for a siesta; B does not feel the heat and insists on sleeping late. A instinctively complies with regulations, B instinctively defies them. A finds it impossible to pass a temple, B finds it impossible to pass a bar. . . .

For Fleming and Maillart, though, even traveling alone was no good if they weren't headed someplace strange and exotic, the more difficult to get to the better. "The trouble about journeys nowadays is that they are easy to make but difficult to justify," Fleming wrote in his introduction to *Tartary.* "The earth, which once danced and spun before us as alluringly as a celluloid ball on top of a fountain in a rifle-range, is now a dull and vulnerable target." But trying to make it from Peking to India across Chinese Turkistan was a challenge that, even in the horribly modern era of the mid-1930s, could capture the imagination of a restless traveler.

In January of 1935, Fleming and Maillart both washed up in Peking after long journeys—solo, of course —through the East. Each was ready to return to Europe, and each had the rather absurd notion of traveling overland through Western China into India. Depending on the exact route, it was a 3,500-to-5,000-mile trip across the sort of territory boys' adventure stories relished labeling "barren and inhospitable." They were headed toward Xinjiang province, "the last home of romance in international politics," Fleming wrote. "Intrigue, violence, and melodrama have long been native to the Province. . . . The Province is at the best of times difficult of access, being surrounded on three sides by mountain ranges whose peaks run well over 20,000 feet, and on the fourth side by the Gobi and the wastes of Mongolia." In difficulty and length, the journey had a striking resemblance to the Long March led by Mao Zedong in 1934. Ninety thousand troops started; twenty thousand finished.

"As a matter of fact, I'm going back to Europe by that route," Fleming announced to Maillart in Peking. This was after she had confided her idea of crossing Turkistan on the way back to Europe. "You can come back with me if you like."

"I beg your pardon," she answered, "it's my route and it's I who will take you, if I can think of some way in which you might be useful to me."

You had to like this pair.

Chapter Two

Behind the Great Wall Sheraton Hotel in Beijing, there is a large park. When looking down from one of the hotel's glass elevators, which slide up and down the exterior of the hotel like zippers, this park looks exactly like a miniature golf course.

During my first few days in Beijing I had been puzzling over the park, trying to remember what it reminded me of. And then I overheard two large men in Iowa State windbreakers talking in the elevator.

"Wanna play a little putt-putt?" One of the men elbowed the other, pointing down.

It really did look like an absolutely first-rate course. There was a little dragon with a wide, open mouth to putt through, a waterfall, several intriguing miniature pagodas, and a couple of rock gardens that would have made ferocious roughs. All that was lacking was a windmill. Windmill obstacles are the toughest shots in putt-putt. I know a girl from Mississippi who concentrated so hard in trying to time her shot to pass through the blades of a windmill obstacle that she became dizzy and fell over, breaking her wrist. Afterward, walking out of the emergency room of the Baptist Hospital, she swore that she was giving up high-risk sports.

Americans, with which the Sheraton is naturally full, look down on the park behind the hotel in amusement. The Chinese do not understand this. There are no miniature golf courses in China—yet. What the Chinese find astonishing and amusing—for good reason—is the Sheraton itself.

A collection of flashing glass cylinders, it rises out of the rubble of northeast Beijing like a UFO. It is only a short walk from the People's Agricultural Hall, a convenience utilized by few guests. But the shuttle bus to the downtown Friendship Store is very popular.

It's not surprising that many of the foreigners who come to the Sheraton embrace shopping at the huge Friendship Store, the government-sponsored (a description easy to overuse in China) department store, with a mad glee. Most are first-time visitors and, for reasons that surely have more to do with the Beijing of 1887 than 1987, they expect to find a pleasing Oriental capital of beauty and charm. What they discover is a nightmare metropolis, a city that gives every impression of striving valiantly to recover from a great and devastating assault.

It makes perfect sense that shopping becomes a passion for the Beijing visitor. It is something to *do* in a city that spent ten years and countless man-hours destroying its temples, museums, and parks; in which restaurants close at 7:00 P.M. and an upcoming Chinese production of *The Music Man* is hailed as proof art is still alive in China.

We—Mark, Fran, David, and I—were in Beijing, because Fleming and Maillart began their journey there. Our goals were simple: rest up from the thirty-hour flight and give away some skis.

"Skis. My God, you've come to China with skis," the assistant manager of the Sheraton gawked as we dragged ourselves off the plane from Tokyo into the splendors of the Great Wall's six-story lobby.

"Yes." I was very tired.

"You plan to ski in China?" His tone was more hopeful than skeptical. He had been in Beijing long enough to wish desperately that there was some fantastic Sino skiing he had somehow overlooked.

"Maybe. Most of these skis I'm giving away."

"Giving away? But who wants skis in a country with no ski areas?"

The logic of this seemed overwhelming. In my jet-lag daze, I tried to assemble an answer. The skis, I finally explained, were for the Chinese Ski Association.

"There *is* a Chinese Ski Association?" the manager asked.

There was, and I had arranged a meeting with them for a couple of reasons. First, I was honestly curious about skiing in China and hoped to wrangle an invitation to race with the Chinese team. But more deviously, I wanted to get a letter from the ski association bestowing their good graces on our venture, something that later we might be able to wave at a Public Security Bureau official when we were trying to get permission to travel into a closed area. I had a feeling that little pieces of paper might prove to be very important down the road.

I had brought the skis that had so amazed the Sheraton staff as a gift. "I bet those boys haven't seen anything like this," David predicted, balancing a pair of super-light Karhu racing skis on two fingers.

"Absolutely," I agreed. "And don't forget the Polaroids. That's sure to wow them." We planned to take some Polaroids of the ski association officials with their new skis.

Before our meeting, Mark explained to me the very specific etiquette of such a Chinese gathering. We were having breakfast in the coffee shop of the Great Wall Sheraton. Mark spent a lot of time here eating prodigiously. When we kidded him, he would shake his head and assert, "But you guys don't know what the food is like out there." "Out there" was non-Beijing China, and he was right. Later, I had memories of the steak and eggs that were positively pornographic.

Mark Salzman knew the world beyond the Sheraton coffee shop because he had lived in China for two years while teaching English and studying wushu, a martial arts discipline. While planning my trip, I'd read his book, *Iron and Silk,* and admired it. Looking for an interpreter, I'd called him to ask if he knew anyone fluent in Chinese I might convince to come with me.

"I might do it," he an wered.

"But I got the impression from *Iron and Silk* that you didn't really like China."

"I don't."

"And that you don't enjoy traveling."

"I think that's right."

When I visited Mark at his apartment a few days later, I began to understand why he might be anxious to leave. It was in the heart of Connecticut's New Haven ghetto, a crumbling brick building with a glass-strewn front yard.

I'd expected a big burly guy along the lines of Chuck Norris. Instead I found somebody who looked like a punk gymnast.

He was short but clearly very powerful with the kind of lithe strength that is so often described by allusions to exotic animals, like cheetahs and jaguars. There wasn't much hair on his head, but what he had stood straight up at odd angles, reminiscent of the drawings in household safety books detailing the effects of finger insertion in electrical outlets.

"Look, I've got to ask, don't you have any problems living in this place?"

"Problems?" Mark has a smile that makes him look not a day over twelve.

"Getting mugged, you know. That stuff."

"I used to but then I started doing some of my routines in the building."

"Routines?"

"Wushu routines."

"Oh."

"The only problem is, I need a lot of room. See . . ." He produced from a corner of his apartment what looked like an overgrown golf bag. He unzipped it to reveal an astonishing array of bizarre weapons.

"I've been working with this a lot lately." He whipped out a five-foot saber with a quickness and grace that was difficult to believe. "But I use each of them every day—the halberd, the long stick, the whip —"

"Whip?"

"A nine-section whip." He reached into the bag for a jumble of metal that resembled automobile snow chains.

"That's a whip?"

"Sure." He stepped into the hall, and with a snake-quick flick of his wrist, he transformed the ball of chain into what looked like a seven-foot steel rod topped by a bright cloth.

A couple stuck their heads out of a door down the hall. Like me, their eyes were wide with awe.

"I can see why you don't get bothered too much."

Mark agreed to accompany me as translator and de facto Chinese expert, helping with delicate questions of protocol—like how to deal with the ski association.

His advice was very specific.

"At the beginning, before you get down to business, you have to give a little speech."

"A speech?" I asked. "In front of two people?" I was to meet Pan Wei Men, the head of winter sports for China, and one of his cross-country ski coaches.

"I know it sounds dumb, but this is what these people expect. It's protocol."

"What do I say?"

"Something like," he sat upright in his chair and folded his hands in front of him. He talked in a curious, upbeat voice with a fixed smile. "I would like to take this opportunity to thank the Chinese Ski Association and its very capable representatives for meeting here today. There are many differences between our countries, but I believe we both share a love for sport. It is possible that here today, through an exchange of ideas and friendship, we can bring our countries closer together through a love for skiing. . . ." He continued on in the same vein for another five minutes.

"Wow."

"Now I think it's important you shouldn't meet them in your room. That's too informal."

I nodded.

"We'll have the meeting in the coffee shop. We can order tea. You always need tea for these things."

"Right." I thought I had read that somewhere before.

"You should introduce me as your official interpreter. I'll say a few words in Chinese and tell them that you are our Little Group Leader."

"Little Group Leader?"

"A very important concept. Every group of Chinese must have a Little Group Leader. Every class has a Little Group Leader; every political study group has a Little Group Leader; every work unit is divided into smaller groups—"

"With a Little Group Leader."

"Right."

"I think you ought to explain to them," I suggested, "where we're trying to go and ask them for some kind of letter bestowing their graces."

Mark looked vaguely uneasy but nodded.

Our meeting was scheduled for 10 A.M.; about fifteen

minutes before, I was in my room looking down at the putt-putt course and thinking how I would shoot around the dragon, when somebody knocked on the door. I figured it was Mark, who had said he would come by so we could go downstairs together when our visitors called.

Stuart?" A good-looking Chinese man of about thirty held out his hand. His longish hair was brushed fashionably back off his forehead; he wore a ski jacket I had seen at the Bogner showroom on Madison Avenue for $250. "Pan Wie Men," he said. "How are you doing?"

His English was impeccable. We shook hands, and he introduced his companion, an older, kindly-looking fellow dressed in a tweed jacket. "This is Li Ting, coach of the cross-country team. Unfortunately, he speaks no English."

Pan started to come into the room. "I thought we should go downstairs," I said, trying to be friendly but formal.

"Oh, this is fine, man" Pan answered, smiling. "We can talk here."

Man, I thought. He said, *man.*

"No, really." I found myself moving in front of him, remembering Mark's instructions. "I think it would be nicer downstairs in the coffee shop. We can have tea." I threw the last bit in desperately to counter the confused look in Pan's eyes.

"Well . . ." he mumbled, and then Fran and David walked out of the bathroom behind me. Pan broke into a grin and gave me a knowing "We men of the World" look. "Of course, we will meet downstairs."

While Fran and David hung up the clothes they had just washed, I dashed to the phone and called Mark. "He came straight up to the room! He didn't call from the lobby."

"Who?"

"The ski guy." I suddenly couldn't remember Pan Wei Men's name. "Both of them."

"That's odd," Mark mused. "But you told them to go back downstairs so we could meet in the coffee shop?"

"Yes, but —"

"No problem. I'll meet you there."

When we were all arranged around one of the Formica tables in the coffee shop, Pan smiled and asked, "So, what part of the States are you from?"

"Maine," Fran answered.

"Mississippi," David said.

Mark gave me an urgent look, nodding forcefully. I swallowed nervously and began my rehearsed speech.

"As American skiers, we are very pleased to have this opportunity to engage in a constructive dialogue with our Chinese friends. There are many differences between our countries but perhaps today, this morning, we can begin to bridge the gap between the two great nations of America and China. Even with an activity as simple as skiing . . ." I was speaking in the same odd tone Mark had adopted; I sounded like a synthesized voice from a high-tech Coke machine. Across from me, Pan Wei Men stared in shock.

"Even with a simple activity like skiing . . ." It was no good. I couldn't do it. Everyone looked at me. The silence was terrible. It suddenly struck me that the coffee shop was decorated in an "Orient Express" theme. Why? Had the Orient Express ever come to Beijing? I knew it hadn't but . . .

Fran eventually broke the silence. "There is skiing in Maine," she said.

"Not in Mississippi," David added, laughing and looking at me as if I had just sprouted chopsticks out of my ears.

"You are a very young man to have such an important position," Mark said to Pan. Mark had told me that they—the Chinese—like to hear that sort of thing.

"Not so young, man. Thirty-five."

Mark laughed. It was an odd, hearty noise, patently false, that sounded like it had been made a long time ago and then frozen. It was nothing at all like Mark's normal laugh, though I had heard him use it before when speaking with Chinese.

Pan and I started talking about the current state of Chinese skiing.

"We train each year in Austria," he explained.

This surprised me.

He went on to explain that the team had a steady supply of first-rate Austrian equipment.

Suddenly my gift skis looked less potent.

I like to ski and can talk about it in a detailed manner that will drive most normal people to distraction. Pan Wei Men and I did just that, covering such fascinating topics as pole length, waxes, and bindings.

Finally David nudged Mark, who unfolded a map and began talking in a bright, happy voice. Like his Chinese laugh, his voice took on an unnaturally upbeat tone, a cross between a salesman and an Ole Miss sorority girl meeting her boyfriend's parents. He smiled ferociously.

Tracing our route, he talked about how difficult it might be to make the trip and how sometimes local authorities were hesitant to give foreigners permission to travel in certain areas because they were—understandably, of course—unfamiliar with what sort of person they were dealing with.

"Where are you going?" Pan Wie Men asked. Though Mark bounced back and forth between Chinese and English, Pan Wie Men stuck determinedly to English.

"Kashgar," Mark answered.

Pan Wie Men looked puzzled.

"Kashi?" Mark tried the Chinese name. "Kasha?" He played around with different pronunciations.

Pan Wie Men nodded knowingly, looking furtively at the map. Mark discreetly pointed to Kashgar.

"It is very far away from Beijing," Mark added helpfully. "Almost all the way to Afghanistan. And we want very much to go a certain way, along the southern edge of the Takla Makan desert."

Pan Wie Men nodded again, this time more hesitantly. He glanced over at me with a confused look, and I tried to smile reassuringly.

"But you cannot ski in the desert," Pan Wie Men eventually said.

Mark explained that we intended to leave our skis in Beijing. "We are concerned about getting permission from the Public Security Bureau for our trip. It can be so helpful just to have some way of letting them know that we are not the sort of Westerners who would cause trouble. If the Public Security Bureau knows we are friends of China, this is a great help."

Pan nodded. He leaned back in his chair putting his hands in his Bogner ski jacket. A certain understanding passed across his eyes.

Mark continued to make broad hints at our needs. Pan continued to nod and say nothing.

It did not look promising. I wanted to barge in and blurt, "Look, what we want you to do is give us a letter so that some frightened official down the road might be more inclined to let us do what we want to do. We'll give you some skis and a Polaroid or two, and we'll all be happy." But what did I know about China?

So I remained quiet. But after another fifteen minutes of hints and feints deftly ignored, I couldn't take it anymore and stood up. Pan jumped to his feet looking relieved. Everyone shook hands, grinning athletically.

In the lobby of the hotel, I presented our gift skis to Pan and the cross-country coach; they seemed to accept them with just enough grace not to embarrass us silly Westerners. Mark took a Polaroid of them with the skis and presented it with a certain flourish. It was a cheap Polaroid, and they seemed to view it with disdain. More handshakes. My face was beginning to ache from smiling. Finally they left. Mark walked with them to the lobby door.

"It's important to escort them out," he said.

Chapter Three

I grew up in a family whose concept of an adventure was not confirming hotel reservations. In writing. Preferably twice.

My mother loved the *idea* of traveling as much as she disliked the reality of where marriage had brought her—Jackson, Mississippi. The latter seemed to propel the former, and our house was always filled with brochures, magazines, and newsletters hailing the delights of exotic places.

Fortunately she came to realize fairly early that reading about horrible places like Peru was much more fun than actually going there. After one exploration to a remote fishing camp in the then wilds of Florida, my father announced that as far as these beautiful, unspoiled places were concerned, he'd just as soon go back when they spoiled them a little more. This excellent advice was taken to heart, and our family safaris were henceforth restricted to outposts such as Sea Island, Georgia, and Grand Hotel, in Point Clear, Alabama.

It was at such places, usually hiding out from a gawky teenager with the title "activity director," that I developed a love for adventure-travel writing. And while the appeal of some ventures faded—I no longer wanted to get a bowl haircut and set out around the world on a tramp steamer as Richard Halliburton had done in *The Royal Road to Romance*—thoughts of *News From Tartary* continued to slink around my brain, seductive and unrepentant.

The Communists had clamped the door on western China in 1949, and only in the last year or so had it become possible to enter that huge region. It was a part of the globe so remote from Beijing that it had no business being called China. Chinese Turkistan—or Tartary—was what it had been known as for centuries, and it was hard to imagine how even the most ardent Communist conformity could have homogenized this vast and fierce territory. Though the Han Chinese—the people with the round faces and narrow eyelids that most of us think of as "true" Chinese—constitute over ninety-eight percent of China's total population, out west they are still a minority. (A situation, I'd learn, they are hard at work to change.) Chinese Turkistan had always been the land of Uighur, Kazakh, Mongol, and Hui tribesmen, some of the earth's great nomads and fighters.

Turkistan is a wild, contradictory territory containing the earth's highest point—Qomolangma, or Mount Everest—and the second lowest point on dry land—the Turfan Depression, 154 meters below sea level. Jammed in between two vast mountain ranges, there is the Takla Makan desert (a name roughly translated as "you go in but do not return"), incongruous swamps, and miles of high, grass-covered steppes that roll monotonously toward the horizon—or so I had heard.

In 1936 Peter Fleming said Turkistan was an area about which little more is known than Darkest Africa. Now all that was changing; but it was still, I reckoned, a place worth seeing, and I wanted to get there before Malcolm Forbes arrived with his motorcycles, TV crews, and French chefs.

When I called Ella Maillart, still very much alive in Geneva, to tell her of my plans to travel in her footsteps, she scoffed. "You must be a very foolish and very young boy."

"Why?" I asked.

"Everything is modern and terrible now."

I thought about this as we gathered our bags to leave the glass and steel Sheraton. There was a slight military feeling to our preparations. David and I wore green wool army fatigues; he had a couple of water bottles hanging from his belt and carried a duffel bag. Even without the pants and gear, David looked like he should belong to some elite special forces unit. His hair was about a week beyond a crew cut, and he had on a Marine Corps Marathon T-shirt under his jacket. He was in intimidatingly good shape; marathons and triathlons were his idea of relaxation. Before taking off from Kennedy he had announced in the most genuinely off-hand manner that he planned to do 1,000 push-ups on the plane just to stave off restlessness.

I'd met David ten years before when we both worked for the same gubernatorial candidate in Mississippi. We lost. David was quiet and very smart, with a stoic sort of love for the physical punishment of eighteen-hour campaign days in Mississippi's 100 degree heat.

In 1984 when I had embarked on a crazy project to ski a record number of international, long-distance races, David volunteered to come with me as coach and logistics chief. He had to cancel at the last minute but promised, "The next weird thing you do, I'm coming. No matter what."

China was the next weird thing.

It was just going to be the three of us—David, Mark, and I—until a few weeks before we planned to leave I got a call from a friend in Washington.

"I've got a wacky question for you."

"Um?"

"What if Fran wanted to go to China with you?"

He was right. It was a wacky question. Fran was Fran Trafton, a young woman who worked for him. I'd only met her once but remembered that she was tall and thin and that everyone in Washington seemed to think she was beautiful.

"I think she's tired of me," my friend told me when I asked why Fran wanted to go. And when I asked him how she might handle the difficulties of the journey, he said very reassuringly, "She's from Maine."

"Maine," I said.

"That means she's used to cold weather. China is cold, right?"

"Yes, it is," I answered, still resolutely unconvinced.

"And she's a great rower. A national champion in college."

This had a certain appeal. Ella Maillart was on the Swiss national sailing team. Fran was a champion rower. We were traveling through a massive desert. It made a certain kind of sense that she should come.

Before I invited her, I called David for his opinion.

He was noncommittal until he heard about her athletic interests.

"Maybe we could train together if she went," he suggested.

"I'm sure she'd enjoy it."

"I tell you what, ask her if she wants to train together and if she says yes, let's bring her."

I didn't do this. Instead, I called my friend and told him she could come.

"So what do you think about going to China?" I asked Fran when she phoned me later.

"Cool. Very cool," she replied.

Oh, God, I thought, what have I done?

But my panicked vision of touring China with a Valley Girl was quickly dispelled our first days in Beijing. And while Fran's rowing skills had yet to be utilized, her background of cold weather had proved imperative. China was the coldest place I'd ever been.

> The Polar Continental air mass, originating in Siberia or Mongolia, dominates a large part of China during the winter. . . . The Siberian air mass is stable and extremely cold and dry. . . . Wind velocities in the winter monsoon, which prevails from November to March, are rather high . . . the cold is often unbearable.

Before leaving America, I'd read all this cheery stuff in a book called *China: Essays on Geography.* But somehow it hadn't made much of an impression during a New York summer.

Standing in front of the Great Wall Sheraton at dusk, eyes tearing from the wind and cold, it became a more personal matter. My God, I thought, if Beijing is like this, what would it be out west?

> A large part of the Quinhai[Qinghai]-Tibet Plateau itself consists of cold deserts. . . . Because of the severe cold and aridity, reclamation of the land is seriously handicapped. . . . Furthermore, as the air is rarefied, human activities are greatly hindered.

The Qinghai-Tibet Plateau was where we were headed.

Chapter
Four

We left Beijing on the night train to Xi'an.
The central train station in Beijing is an immense, extraordinarily confusing place. I liked it immediately. There were escalators that didn't work and stairs rising in every direction. Impossibly long lines wove intricate patterns throughout the station, like snakes coiled at the bottom of a basket. The lines were single file until they neared the tiny ticket windows where all order collapsed and they took on the aggressive chaos of a rugby scrum. The light was vague, the noise terrific.

I had the feeling we had stumbled into the midst of an urgent evacuation from an impending disaster. There was a powerful Last-Chopper-Out-Of-Saigon feel to the place. It was difficult to believe that this same scene would be reenacted again tomorrow night and the next and the next and . . .

We walked up the broken escalator for a long time, through a dim hall and then descended another preposterously long staircase to the track. I was sweating, my back hurting from the strap of my luggage. The pushing and shoving was constant. But no one seemed to mind when you pushed back. I did this a lot.

When we reached the bottom of the stairs at the track level, I saw something I'd wanted to see all my life: steam engines, five or six of them, in regular use. I stopped, buffeted by the rushing Chinese, and gawked. The machines were huge and beautiful, with gleaming pistons, bright steel flashing against the blackness of the engine body. Moving over the tracks with great deliberation, they seemed to embody the very essence of power. Great clouds of steam rose into the cold night air. It was all very joyful.

The soft sleeper car was conveniently positioned close to the bottom of the stairs. We struggled aboard and found the car filled with People's Liberation Army officers and prosperous-looking party cadres.

There were six, four-person berths in the car. A dirty red carpet ran down the aisle; a thin green one covered the floor of the compartment. Thick cotton quilting lay in rolls at the end of each bed; the mattresses were wrapped in a grayish white sheet, held in place by snaps and decorated with a row of fringe. It was cozy and surprisingly warm.

A Chinese version of "Jingle Bells" bounced over the train speakers. A plump, smiling conductress carried in four lidded mugs and a handful of tea bags. She pointed out the large thermos of hot water nestled under the compartment table. It was bright pink and decorated with frisky-looking bunny rabbits hoping every which way. HIPPITY HAPPY POT it read in English.

"What is she saying?" I asked Mark, indicating the chirpy voice that followed "Jingle Bells" over the loudspeaker.

"Comrades, we welcome you to your journey. Do not spit everywhere . . ."

In the dining car a woman from Los Angeles was surrounded by a group of Chinese men—train conductors and PLA soldiers. They had been drinking and the men, intoxicated by the Bajo, the clear 99 proof liquor, and the presence of a lone, drunken Western woman, pressed close, giggling. "Happy Thanksgiving!" she shouted at me, downing more Bajo.

I glanced at a calendar on the rocking dining car wall. It featured a painting of a Chinese woman with an unnaturally large bust holding a young boy. "She is a good comrade!" the inscription read. "She has one child!" I counted back the days since arriving in Beijing.

"Happy Thanksgiving," I answered.

The woman was in her late thirties and once, perhaps, she had been very pretty. She was dressed with curious formality in black high heels and an attractive gray wool business suit. She must have been accustomed to a very different sort of suitor than this crush of Chinese men, who interrupted their giggling and drinking to spit raucously on the dining car floor. But this Thanksgiving evening she seemed quite grateful for the attention. The lights flickered on and off as the train picked up speed south of Beijing. I felt embarrassed, as if I had interrupted a sexual act.

Later, I heard her high debutante laugh float by our compartment. Guided by PLA soldiers, she disappeared into the darkness of the hard-class sleeper car. Though I watched at every stop, I never saw her again.

A maintenance man appeared in the doorway of our compartment. He carried twin flashlights he twirled like six shooters. Sitting down next to me, he squeezed my arm. Once. Twice. I was wearing a short-sleeve shirt, and his grip was firm against my skin.

How strong was I? he asked.

Why?

He laughed softly, and then his eye caught a Polaroid of Fran propped up on the little table next to the window. It had been taken while she was pulling off a sweater, and the glimpses of her bare shoulders and arms made her appear half-nude. The maintenance man, number 1461 of the Railway Work Unit, stared at the photo, aiming one of his flashlight beams at it. His hand still gripped my arm. He did this for a very long time until Mark said something to him in Chinese, and he suddenly left.

"What did you tell him?" Fran, who had been blushing, asked Mark.

"That we were having a political study session."

"Oh."

"I said I was the Little Group Leader." Mark smiled.

"What were we studying?"

"Reagan-thought."

We went to sleep.

That night as a huge steam engine roared by, pistons flashing, I woke up in the blackness of the compartment, sweating under the thick cotton quilt, and wondered where I was.

Chapter
Five

The sun came up the next morning over a jumbled landscape of smokestacks. I sat in the dining car of the train, shivering.

There is a game everyone who has ridden a train in winter has played: sitting warm and cozy inside, you look out and wonder how cold it really is out there. The Beijing to Xi'an dining car provided an easy answer—the inside of the train was the same temperature as outside. Or close enough to reverse the speculation. I found myself watching the peasants walking by the track in the early sun jealously pondering how much warmer they were than I.

But there was something about the dining car that was very pleasing. It didn't have the streamlined, efficient design that has made eating in trains in America and too often in Europe a numbing, unpleasant task. This car was cluttered and decidedly silly.

Two round, glass columns like barber poles were mounted over every window. I suppose they were lights, but I never saw them illuminated. Dirty blue curtains, the curtains of a little girl's playhouse, hung frozen by frost to the windows. Every table held a cluster of plastic flowers in a blue-patterned vase. The seats were metal folding chairs with red cloth draped over them. Unattached to the floor, they rattled when empty, skidded precariously when occupied. The tables were covered in dirty plastic.

Red cloth banners urging SERVE THE PEOPLE hung on the wall and over the door. They looked worn and tired, like fading tapestries saved from another era. At the last table in the car, a pyramid of beer cans swayed continuously but inexplicably never fell. Chinese disco music bounced in over the loudspeakers. This was the stuff that only a few years ago could get a listener arrested. Perhaps that's why, long suppressed, disco seems to be an overwhelming favorite with the female conductors who run the little disc jockey booths on the trains. Despite the abrasive but catchy beat, no one ever responded in the slightest to the rhythms, no nodding of heads or tapping of feet, not even a hum or two.

David and I had a breakfast of noodles in a clear broth that tasted of fish. It was peculiar but warm.

I stirred my noodles and watched two men running downhill alongside an ox cart piled high with cabbages. One man was trying to grab the ox, a not very promising endeavor, and the other had latched onto the rear of the cart, pulling backward with no visible effect. The cart teetered and tilted, gathering speed, until it finally tumbled all the way over, spilling everything—the cabbages, the men, and the ox—explosively in different directions. I could hear the ox bellowing.

All at once there was a mad rush of people from the direction of the hard-seat cars. The diner was jammed in seconds. This diving for seats was carried out in total silence with an adeptness that indicated long practice. I wondered if perhaps the Chinese Communists, with their love of all things military, had elevated dining car seating to a strict precision, like the silent Marine drill team in America.

"Look, there," David nodded across the car to a man who stared straight ahead; his hair stood on end, and he had the glumness of a man who wasn't ready to face the morning without his proper share of fish noodles. I was completely sympathetic.

"That fellow could be an Apache. Absolutely."

"Apache?"

David laughed and nodded. I had to admit that the more I stared at the man the more he began to take on certain Geronimo-like characteristics. This worried me.

As if to augment my confusion, the PA system shifted abruptly from disco to a dramatic martial tone. It rose in volume from the merely loud to the painful.

Our dining companions twisted to look ahead out the windows. Some actually smiled.

"What's happening?" David asked.

A female announcer's voice joined the loud music.

"It's the Yellow River," a young man at the next table said in English.

"What's she saying?" I asked, indicating the loudspeaker.

He shrugged. "She is talking about how the Yellow River is the mother of China." The man, about twenty-five or so, wore thick, black glasses; he had one of those exaggerated faces—teeth jutting out, eyes bulging behind myopic lenses—that seemed more like a caricature than a real person. He reminded me of Jerry Lewis imitating a Chinaman.

"The mother of China," David said. "We have a river like that in America."

"Oh, yes, of course," our friend agreed, nodding vigorously.

"We do?" I asked.

"It's called the Mississippi."

The river below us was four or five hundred yards wide and looked very shallow, with wide sandbanks stretching out on either shore. Steep bluffs rose suddenly out of the sand.

It was a calm stretch of water, but I knew that not far from here the river had participated in horrendous violence. The story I'd read about it seemed like one of those confluences of natural and man-made disasters that flourish in China.

In 1938, at the height of the spring floods, Chiang Kai-shek ordered the bombing of the dykes of the Yellow River just north of Zhengzhou. He did it to interrupt the advance of the invading Japenese army, something his own troops hadn't been able to do. The stratagem worked, at least for a few weeks, but it killed upward of a million Chinese in the process and left another 10 million homeless with no means of feeding themselves.

The unchecked flooding was repeated each spring until American aid and advisors helped rebuild the dykes in 1947. It is said that an early slogan of Chairman Mao was inscribed in the embankment: "Control the Yellow River."

"I am studying in America," the man said. He did not appear very interested in the mother of China.

"Where?" David asked.

"The University of Minnesota. Agronomy. I am an agronomist."

His name was Wu Jan Ming. We talked about Minnesota for a while, and then I said, "You know, I would like very much to hear more about the Red Guard."

The agronomist fixed his head to the side and gave me a wacky, toothy look that seemed to register surprise.

This wasn't the first time in China I had tried to talk to someone about the Red Guard and the Cultural Revolution. In Beijing, Mark and I spent an afternoon wandering around the Forbidden City and fell into a conversation with a pair of amiable PLA soldiers. It was a cloudy, bitterly cold day, and we had stopped at a little stand selling sweetened hot milk. The soldiers spoke a few words of English, just enough to start a dialogue but hardly adequate to progress beyond the "How many years do you have?" stage. They were from Beijing, about our age, and I was curious to know what had happened to the Forbidden City during the Cultural Revolution. Obviously it had been protected by troops (allegedly under the direction of Chou En-lai), but I wanted more details. Had the Red Guard tried to enter? Was there a battle? Had these two soldiers, who would have been the right age, been part of the Red Guard? These were nosy but not, I thought, outrageous questions.

"I can't ask that," Mark said.

"Why?"

"It's embarrassing. I mean, what if they don't want to talk about it?"

"Let's try at least."

"You do it," Mark answered.

"But I don't speak Chinese!"

Mark smiled apologetically and shrugged.

But the agronomist spoke excellent University of Minnesota English.

"It must have been a very difficult time during the Cultural Revolution," I ventured.

"Yes, very hard, very hard. Many bad things happened."

"What do you remember?"

"I was very young. But in my village, I can remember fighting." His voice had lowered; his eyes shifted around the diner.

"Fighting between whom?"

The young man shrugged. "Sometimes the Red Guard and police, some time the Red Guard with each other."

"If the Red Guard did so many bad things, why didn't the people fight back?"

34

"It was difficult," he finally said after a pause. Then unexpectedly, "America, I like it very much."

"How long have you been at the University of Minnesota?"

"Two years. I have three more for my doctorate degree."

"Are you home for Christmas holidays?" It struck me that our conversation was beginning to sound like two Fitzgerald characters riding a train from Princeton to New York.

He shook his head. "It is my mother, she is very ill." He smiled apologetically.

"I'm sorry."

"I think this may be the last chance I have to see her." I didn't say anything.

"I expected not to see her for five years, all the time I am in America. But then the sickness. It is cancer. In the stomach." He rubbed his stomach.

"Does your family live in Xi'an?"

"No, Ürümqi. At the end of the train line. It is two days and two nights after Xi'an."

"Are there many Hans in Ürümqi?"

"Now there are. When we first came there from Hunan, when I was very young, there were not so many."

"Why did your family want to move to Ürümqi?"

Wu Jan Ming smiled. "My father was sent. They needed doctors."

"Does he like it?"

"Now, it is not so bad. But at first it was terrible."

"Why?"

"Ürümqi is a hard place, very hard. There was nothing there," he laughed, "nothing at all. Only Uighurs and donkeys."

Ürümqi and Kashgar were the two major towns in the province of Xinjiang. The relationship between the

Han Chinese—Wu Jan Ming's people—and the indigenous population had long been a violent one. Fleming wrote:

> The name Sinkiang (Hsin Chiang) means the New Dominion; but China has curious standards of novelty, and she originally conquered the Province in the first century B.C. Her hold however was not at that time firmly established and successive waves of conquest —Huns, Tibetans, Mongols under Chinghis Khan and Tamerlane—ebbed and flowed over territory which was for centuries important because it carried the overland route between the West and the Far East, the great Silk Road. In the latter half of the eighteenth century the massacre of over a million of the inhabitants celebrated the more or less definitive reassertion of Chinese rule, and in spite of recurrent rebellions throughout the nineteenth century, culminating in the temporary domination of Kashgaria by the adventurer Yakub Beg, Sinkiang formed part of the Chinese Empire during the last 150 years of its existance.

When Fleming wrote his description in 1935, Chinese control of Xinjiang (or Sinkiang) was tenuous. The total population was, as Fleming described it, "Turkis [Uighurs] (who form about seventy per cent of the whole), Mongols, a few Kirghiz and Tadjiks, Tungans," with only "small communities of Chinese merchants and administrators, and soldiers. . . ." Since then, the Han Chinese in Xinjiang have increased to more than 13 million, a two-to-one dominance over all other races. The Beijing government has labeled all non-Hans—of which Uighurs, a blue-eyed stock of Moslem tribesmen, are the most numerous—official "minorities, part of the great Chinese family," as one official pamphlet put it.

I asked my friend if he planned to live in Ürümqi.

"Probably. It is part of the reason I was sent to America to study. They need agronomist in Xinjiang Province. They will keep me there, I think."

"The government?"

"It is different in America." He sounded both apologetic and sad.

"Do you think about staying in America?" I asked. The Chinese government admits that about half the students it allows to study in America do not return to China. Some have said the number is actually closer to eighty percent.

"My family is here," he answered quietly. His face seemed less comic now.

A waiter in a dirty, white smock with a pocketful of chopsticks motioned brusquely for everyone to leave. There was another crowd waiting at the door for their noodles.

"I hope your mother does better," I said lamely, as we shook hands.

"She will die," he answered levelly, "but I will see her first. That is all I can ask for."

"There was a kind of prehistoric look about this land, through which the train snorted laboriously, like an antediluvian monster." So Fleming described the area west of the Yellow River. With his prehistoric musings, he seemed to be thinking about cavemen; David had other ideas.

"Indians," David pronounced. "Pueblo Indians. Look at those caves."

I looked. We were moving through an extraordinary landscape. Cliffs, riddled with caves, rose on both sides of the train—a whole city of caves. Some of the cave entrances were faced with brick, their archways decorated with a red star. Others were unadorned holes cut into the clay walls.

They did look like something you might see in Arizona. Except for the red stars, of course.

"Many people live in these caves," a man said, looking out the window with us in the corridor. His hair was laced with gray and he wore two sweaters, a white shirt, a jacket, and heavy, gray pants. It was cold in the corridor. He had metal glasses and the face of a pleasing older uncle.

"How many do you think?" David asked.

He shook his head. "Numbers are very difficult in China. Millions. Millions." (Later, I read that some 100 million—almost half the population of America—were cave dwellers.)

We looked out the window. I thought the caves looked warm and inviting, surprisingly unbleak. As a little boy I had been regaled with the story of relatives who had lived in caves during the siege of Vicksburg. Naturally it had sounded romantic and daring and had given me, I suppose, a certain predilection toward cave life.

But I had never lived in a cave. A Chinese writer named Wu Huan had:

> It's just like a devil's lair. A few oil lamps flicker in the gloom like ghosts' eyes. . . . A wooden structure, one huge room seventy or eighty metres long stuck deep in the mountains of Xiaoxing'an. Like a massive burrow. They'd dug into the frozen earth with pickaxes and planted the squared wooden posts, fixing them

in the ground with melted snow. It froze solid
as it was poured around the stakes. . . . No
ordinary place this. Put simply, anyone who
has lived here, even if only for a day, must be
counted a hero, one way or another.

Wu Huan was an "urbling," one of the educated
urban youths forced to live in the countryside during the
Cultural Revolution. The son of a playwright and opera
singer, Wu Huan lived for a decade in the cave he described in his book, *Black Nights, Forest, Dumb Urbling.*

We were at the end of the corridor where the smell
from the toilet competed with the acrid cigarette smoke.
Lu Wei Hong, the man with two sweaters, presented his
card with a formal flourish. Railway Signal Engineer, it
read; one side was in English, the other Chinese. We hit
the usual subjects—where he had been in America
(Rochester, Louisville, Kentucky); the weather (freezing,
of course); Chinese and American trains. And then he
asked if we knew "I-Coke-Ah."

"What's that?" David asked.

Lu Wei Hong smiled broadly. "Let I-Coke-Ah, a big
man. The big man who saved Crystler."

"Lee Iacocca. Yes."

"His biography very impressive. Very strong."

"Did you read it while in America?" David was doing
the questioning.

"Oh, no, my boss told all of us to read it."

"But why? Isn't he a capitalist running dog?" I asked.

I meant this as a joke but Lu Wei Hong's face was
terribly serious.

"Of course. But he is a very good manager. Management very important now in China." His face grew even
sterner. "I think socialist and capitalist can share management techniques."

"Management techniques?"

"Very important to help the people."

"Can you buy Iacocca's book in China?"

"Every day in the *People's Daily*, two pages of the I-Coke-ah book is run."

"That's almost the whole paper."

"Yes. This is very important."

Startling as the idea was, it did make a certain amount of sense that Iacocca would go over big in the country molded by Mao. The two had a lot in common: both were megalomaniacs, and both had a special knack for what might be called Succeeding Through Failure. Mao realized that he was losing his grip in 1965, so he launched the Cultural Revolution and reestablished himself as the dominant figure in China. Iacocca was fired by Ford, landed a job as head of a bankrupt company that made terrible cars, had to beg Congress for a billion dollars—all the sort of stuff that would have made any normal person embarrassed to appear in public. And yet he had the gall to strut around on national television in commercials, becoming a folk hero in the process.

Both were also fashion arbiters in their own right—Mao, the blue jackets and cap; Iacocca, the shirts with contrasting collars and cuffs. And both had been trading for years on one impressive achievement: Mao had pulled off the Long March, and Iacocca had overseen the creation of the Mustang.

Lu Wei Hong talked about the Long March and compared it in significance to the fourth of July and Lincoln's "Gettysburg Address." Then, standing in the swaying train, the Xiao Mountains glowing in the sun, our breath issuing up clouds of steam in the freezing carriage, Hong began to recite the "Gettysburg Address":

"Four score ago our fathers brought forward a nation for the government, by the government—"

"You mean people," David interjected gently. "For the people by the people."

"Oh, yes. Very sorry."

I never thought getting off a train could be confusing. But then I had never gotten off a train in Xi'an, China. It was crazy.

As we stepped onto the track, hundreds of people rushed frantically in one direction, hundreds in another. All points of the compass had their fans. Thick dust swirled everywhere.

Crumbling brick walls topped by barbed wire ringed the station grounds. We stumbled around until we found a line and numbly joined it. Mark looked very glum. He wore a black watch cap pulled low over his ears and dragged his bag behind him as we inched forward.

David, whose disposition seemed to brighten in direct proportion to the unpleasantness of any situation, said something encouraging.

"You know what we're doing?" Mark responded. "We're standing in line so that some old lady can collect our tickets. Now why is this person collecting used tickets? Does it serve any purpose? Does a used ticket have any value? Does this little old lady really care if you have a ticket . . ."

He seemed to feel better as he talked. We finally reached the front of the line where a young woman, not an old one, wanted our ticket.

"Tell her I don't have one, Mark," I said, feeling peevish after the long wait. "I want to see what she will say."

Mark didn't say anything, and I couldn't blame him. I gestured empty handed for the girl and smiled. She didn't smile but looked at me tiredly, with flat eyes, and waved me on. I felt silly but better than I would have if I had routinely handed over the ticket. Behind me others moved through without a ticket as well. The scene had the dreariness of an over-rehearsed play.

Outside in a parking lot lit by a single string of electric bulbs, a flotilla of battered rickshas and Russian taxis waited. It looked strangely like an American used-car lot. We squeezed into a car and headed off.

But not very far. A few hundred yards down a dark road, the car sputtered to a halt. Laughing nervously in that annoying Chinese way, the driver cranked and re-cranked. The starter moaned.

The driver spoke up.

"He thinks it's the oil," Mark translated.

The battery died. We piled out. The driver propped open the hood and stared at the engine. He was tall and skinny and wore round tortoiseshell sunglasses of the sort you might see see on a Yale undergrad at the beach. He gazed down at the engine incredulously, as if seeing for the first time the magic device that ran his chariot.

The dark street was lined with dimly lit shops. High-pitched music floated out from the doorways. Bicycles slipped by in the cold night air like spirits. A sullen crowd gathered to stare. It was a clear night, and looking upward, through the steam of my breath, I could see the Milky Way with perfect clarity.

Above a doorway covered by a blanket, a faded telephone symbol hung by a broken stanchion.

"Let's try and call a hotel," I suggested to Mark. "Maybe they can send another car." Mark nodded, but he had this look he got when he thought one of us had made an utterly preposterous, impossible-to-do-in-China suggestion. I seemed to do this more than anyone.

42

We walked over to the doorway and parted the curtains, blinking in the sudden light. The small room was stacked with bunk beds, an astonishing number of bunk beds in fact, surely a record for bunk beds in one room. In each, under a dirty mound of bedding, a young Chinese boy peered out at us, mouth and eyes gaping. An old lady, shrunken and wearing an apron with Donald Duck on it, sat behind a wobbly desk.

"Telephone?" Mark murmured, too startled by the scene to put on his Happy-Foreigner-So-Glad-To-Be-In-China routine with which he began most requests.

"It doesn't work," she replied, smiling. She reached into a desk drawer and came out with a device that looked like it had been stolen from the People's Communication Museum—The First Telephone. It was big and black and cracked in a dozen places.

Mark dialed a number. "Wei! Wei!" he shouted.

There is a better than average chance that the last words I utter in this world will be "Wei! Wei." Deep in my subconscious the word is irretrievably implanted. While it doesn't exactly translate as "hello," it is the first thing people say over the telephone in China. No, that's wrong. It's the first thing people SHOUT over the phone.

A lot of countries—America is working hard to become one—have nightmarish telephone service. But China's, I believe, is unique in one regard: not only is the audio quality of the tin-can-and-string variety, but somehow the system (a misleadingly official-sounding term) is designed so that if there is more than a few seconds of silence on the line, the connection automatically disconnects. Since getting through in the first place usually takes hours, this is a devastating occurrence. Chinese have conditioned themselves to fight this menace by filling every spare second of conversation with "Wei! Wei!," always shouted at maximum volume to penetrate the melange of static, 1940 radio shows, and random tortured shrieks that drift through every conversation.

Surprisingly, Mark reached the Sportsman Hotel; it was near the town stadium and we wanted to stay there, hoping we might run into some wushu athletes Mark knew. It was full. We called another. No one answered.

When we came out, the driver was doing an astonishing thing. He was attempting to pour gasoline into the car tank using a plastic bag as a funnel. A large crowd offered a cacophony of advice. For a moment I wondered if perhaps this is just the way it's done in China, if every five-gallon gas can came equipped with a baggie.

But if it was a local custom, our driver had not yet mastered its intricacies. He seemed to be doing a much better job of imitating a monk bent on public self-immolation. He reeked of gas, a sizable puddle of which lay under the car. Almost everyone in the crowd was smoking.

David suggested we look for another taxi. We gathered our bags and moved away.

"Do you think that's dog meat?" Fran asked, pointing to a suspicious hunk of raw meat hanging from a bicycle. After wandering through a Beijing market, Fran had developed an unusual interest in dog meat.

We flagged another taxi, evicted the startled passengers, and drove in search of a hotel.

Chapter
Six

I stared at the chart for a long time. It listed which trains to take to reach points west. Ürümqi, Xinning, Lanchow—these were the big towns, the destination of most trains. But written in small letters at the bottom was: Golmud, train 6, Xinning.

The chart was encouraging. And so was its location in the China International Travel Service (CITS) office. Since CITS dealt exclusively with foreigners, it seemed logical to assume that foreigners were allowed to travel to Golmud. Why else would they make the information available?

"It's okay to travel to Golmud?" I asked one of the young men in the office.

Golmud was directly on Fleming's route, perched at the edge of the Takla Makan desert, the jumping off point for the Southern Silk Road.

The official looked at me strangely. "Of course. There is a train."

"How long does it take?"

"Why?" He smiled happily.

"I want to go." I smiled back.

"But you are a foreigner. It can be difficult for foreigners to go to Golmud."

"Do I need a special permit to get to Golmud?" I asked.

"It is possible."

"Can you give me a permit just in case I might need it?"

The idea of this seemed to please him. "Yes, that would be good," he chuckled. "But I cannot do so."

"Why?"

"Golmud is in Qinghai province. You would have to get the permit in that province."

"Oh." There was just enough logic in this to make it really annoying.

"You should stay in Xi'an. Xi'an is nice town. Foreigners like Xi'an. Many foreigners come here now."

This was true. "Next to Beijing, Xi'an is the best city to visit in China, especially if you are interested in ancient Chinese history, traditional culture, and archaeology," says Temple Fielding's 1987 China guide.

When Fleming and Maillart came through Xi'an in 1935, they landed in the middle of a civil war. "The military situation was critical," Maillart later wrote. "Only a few days before, the town had almost fallen into the hands of the Communists. The strain of events weighed all the more heavily on everybody owing to the fact that the town had suffered terribly in the great famine of a few years before . . . the famished population had eaten hundreds of dead every day."

This was altogether not the sort of place Temple Fielding's readers would like to end up. The "critical" military situation Maillart refers to was resolved in bizarre but pleasant circumstances that should certainly be adopted as the preferred way to end all civil wars. Generals on both the Communist and Kuomintang sides realized that if the Japanese were allowed to continue their encroachment into China, it wouldn't really matter who won the civil war: they'd all be serving Japanese masters. The sticking point was the Kuomintang commander-in-chief, Chiang Kai-shek, who was too wrapped up in yet

46

another of his "extermination" campaigns against the Communists—the "National Bandit Suppression Commission" was its official title—to deal with the larger menace of Japanese hegemony.

So Chiang's generals did a very logical thing: they arrested their commander-in-chief at a noted hot springs bathhouse on the outskirts of Xi'an. That Chiang Kai-shek did not have the sensitivity to detect a brewing coup d'etat among his own generals probably goes a long way toward explaining why Chiang ended up in Taiwan and Mao moved into the Forbidden City.

Under arrest, Chiang quickly perceived the wisdom of united Chinese opposition to the Japanese and forged a reluctant partnership with the Communists that lasted, more or less, until after World War II. Then the two sides returned to what each did best: Chiang at generating "anti-bandit" rhetoric and the Communists at winning battles.

There remains in Xi'an today an obscure relic of this awkward Chinese alliance. A liaison office was established between the Communists and Chiang's forces in a walled compound not far from the city center. In 1946 when the Chinese resumed their civil war, the hall was abandoned, but later, after the Communists won, it was reincarnated as a memorial to the Eighth Route Army.

We stumbled across the low mud walls of this building one afternoon riding bicycles. We were lost, but this was nothing new. Our state of orientation continually oscillated between mildly confused and hopelessly, no-idea-where-the-hell-we-were lost. It wasn't just that Mark was the only one of us who could read Chinese. The truth was there weren't many signs—which I suppose makes sense in a country where almost no one can travel. Most of the Chinese know where they are because it's the only place they've ever been.

I was learning in China that being semi-lost is actually a pleasant experience. If nothing else, you feel a sense of gratitude that you're not more severely misplaced. But you also experience a sort of enforced lassitude, because, as in quicksand, dramatic or rapid movements never really pay off when you are trying to get your bearings. There is no point in hurrying from point B to C if you aren't at all sure C is where you want to end up, or for that matter if you aren't sure that C is really C.

In Xi'an we stayed at the Renmin Hotel. Renmin means "people's." It's a word you hear a lot in China. Countless hotels, parks, cars, even money go under the Renmin label.

The Renmin was a wonderful, intricately peculiar place. It was on one of the town's main streets, behind a massive pair of gates of the sort Texans depend on to give their ranches an air of distinction. Beyond the gates, the grounds resembled northern Italy—a long circular driveway wrapped around a park with flashy fountains and even a quaint stone bridge. Then there was Russia.

Seeing a structure like the Renmin and then learning it was built by the Russians is a comforting experience. The place looks so perfectly, stereotypically Russian: huge and brown and awesomely solid.

Tucked away behind the seven-story bulkhead of the Renmin, there's a smaller, newly renovated addition where the hotel puts its "foreign guests." The rooms were modern and comfortable with a hidden entertainment value that surfaced after a night or two. Like those paintings that cleverly conceal hidden objects, each room came equipped with an unusual defect obscured at first glance by the sparkling newness of the renovations. It was great fun to wander the halls peering into the mostly empty rooms trying to guess the special qualities of each. Ingeniously, no two chambers were alike.

"Look, this room is perfect."

"Impossible."

"You're right, there it is, there aren't any curtains."

"Now this one is tricky . . ."

"Turn on the lights so we can see better."

"That's it! There aren't any lights."

I took great pride in asserting that my room was functionally perfect: the lights worked; it had curtains; there were faucets on the fixtures; the toilet seat wasn't missing. (Somebody in China was obviously collecting these.) The only blemish on its impeccable veneer was a missing panel in the bathroom ceiling. I hardly noticed this until an oversized rat fell out of the ceiling hole into my bath late one night. Unfortunately I had trouble mustering a quick defense as the bathwater was precisely the color of the rat, a flat dark brown.

Later I decided to try to avoid this Chinese equivalent of the shower scene in *Pschyo* by planning my ablutions for midday when I figured that rodents, like everyone in the country, would be resting. Of course this dictated a strictly cold-water experience—the hot water appeared, like the rats, only very late at night—but it seemed a more than fair trade-off.

Chapter Seven

T he first thing Peter Fleming did when he arrived in Xi'an was visit a couple of missionaries at the Baptist Hospital. He did this not because he was sick or in need of Christian brotherhood; Fleming was looking to mooch.

The young Englishman was quite good at this. Armed with just the right letter of introduction, he appeared at strange doorsteps all the way to India. Many of these doors were opened by missionaries, a logical enough occurrence since they were often the only Europeans around. And they were also more inclined, one supposes, for reason of professional image if nothing else, to extend hospitality once put on the spot.

Of the two missionaries he and Kini stayed with in Xi'an, Fleming wrote only that they were "charming." But Maillart in her account puts a little more meat on the bones:

> I was chatting with my hostess and it came out that the Mr. Fleming with whom I had arrived was the author of *One's Company*. She was outraged.
>
> "He has a cheek," said she, "to claim hospitality from us after making a mock of missionaries the way he did."

Back when I first considered retracing Maillart and Fleming's trip, I thought there might be a chance of tracking down some missionaries or children of missionaries still in China who would remember the pair. It was a silly idea but then nearly everything about the trip fell into that category.

"We want to declare before the whole world: church and evangelistic work inside China is the right and responsibility of our Chinese Church," Bishop K.H. Ting, the leader of the Christian church in China, announced in his opening remarks at the 1980 Chinese National Christian conference. Bishop Ting made it clear why there were no foreign missionaries in China today: "No people outside China, regardless of the color of their skin, should carry on any activity of a missionary nature inside China or directed at China."

I'd read Bishop Ting's remarks in a report prepared by an Episcopal priest, Patrick Mauney, on the current state of the church in China. An aide to the presiding bishop of the United States, Mauney had recently visited China preparing his study. When I talked with him before leaving the States, he'd explained how the Communists had officially outlawed missionaries shortly after "liberation" in 1949, but then had looked the other way, allowing many to continue operating.

This informal tolerance lasted until the Cultural Revolution when missionaries were hot targets again, just as they had been in 1900 during the Boxer Rebellion. In those days, nothing pleased a xenophobic member of the Society of the Righteous and Harmonious Fist like roasting a missionary over a low fire. Martyrdom not being what it used to be—at least for Christians—the last of the foreign missionaries took the high road out when the first seizures of the Cultural Revolution's mass insanity shook China in 1966.

Since then, churches had reopened although, like everything in the New China, there had to be a political justification, however twisted, for their existence. Bishop Ting:

> Communists know better than anyone else that building up the New China is not only the work of one party, but of all the people. They are uniting all who can be united for the common struggle. Like all their citizens, those who believe in Jesus Christ ardently desire a strong and prosperous motherland . . . it is only natural that Christians are part of the United Front.

This was great stuff, and it made me even more eager to meet some Chinese Christians. I'd heard there was a church in Xi'an—if you could find it.

Somehow we did. It was tucked down an alley not far from the dreary Friendship Store. A tiny red cross was the only indication that this drab brick building might be different from any other. When we pedaled up on our rented bikes around 10:00 A.M., a large crowd was coming out, jamming the narrow alleyway.

We stopped, surprised by the commotion. A beggar—something that is a more common in New York than in China—propped himself on two crude wooden crutches at the edge of the crowd, a ceramic bowl held out in his hand. His feet were twisted inward, useless and clumsy; as if on cue, an old woman hobbled past him on feet mutilated by girlhood binding.

"Where are you from?" a man asked us kindly, stepping forward.

"America."

"Are you Christians?"

This is a question I have never liked, if only because the people who ask it are inclined to be a pushy breed of converts. But this smiling, gentle, middle-aged man seemed genuinely interested, not just feeling us out as possible conquests.

"Yes," Fran answered.

"Then we are brothers in Christ."

He faced me, cocking his head to the side with an inquisitive glimmer in his eyes. *Brothers in Christ.* It was a phrase I had not heard since my Sunday School days in the damp basement of Gallaway Methodist Church in Jackson, Mississippi. We used to say prayers for missionaries in China, and I wondered if one of "ours" had taught this man his simple, strong statement.

"My name is Yu Xu Ling." He took off his thin, blue gloves and held out his hand. Yu Xu Ling was a neat man in clothes that were Western in design but Chinese in construction. Lightly perched on his head was a gray felt fedora with a flat, round brim. A long, white scarf made of some synthetic that felt like it had been woven from the inside of car seats—I had bought one just like it in Beijing—was carefully tucked inside a herringbone coat with a modish collar, not unlike the cut of coat bought by British rock stars in the late sixties on Carnaby Street. His cheekbones were amazingly sharp, jutting out so far they made the bottom half of his face look shrunken. Along with his kindly smile there was a deep tiredness, or maybe sadness, in his eyes.

"Did you come to services today? I did not see you inside."

"No, we just arrived. The church is very hard to find."

"But there are many people on Sunday." He smiled and gestured to the crowd. "How long will you stay in Xi'an?"

I explained that we weren't sure.

"Where do you stay? I would like to meet with you so we could have fellowship in the brotherhood of Christ and I could practice my English."

I wasn't sure I liked either prospect. But it was the first direct request anyone had made of me in China.

We agreed that he would come by my room at the Renmin the following morning. In the background I thought I could hear Mark chortling quietly. After two years in China, he had developed a powerful aversion to what he called "the language rapist" who preyed on Westerners by cornering them and using them like Berlitz Basic English records. I think Mark particularly resented them because he was at heart the quintessential softie—he hated to say no to anyone.

The actual church building was at the end of a passageway leading from the alley. It was a dark, appealing place with dusty brick floors and a high arched roof bisected by rough beams. Narrow rectangular windows granted the only light; two of the windows were filled with a mosaic of colored glass. Wooden pews were jammed tightly together from the rear wall to the foot of the simple altar.

I wandered down the center aisle to get a better look at the altar and began talking to a couple in their late fifties. She was plump and jolly, wearing sharply pointed cat's-eye glasses. I had seen pictures of Peggy Guggenheim wearing a similar pair. The man was quiet, his English not quite as good.

Her father had been a missionary, she explained. She had learned English in the mission school in Shanghai.

I pondered what sort of hell she must have gone through during the Cultural Revolution when any semblance of Western traits was punishable by the most hideous consequences. Pianists routinely had their fingers broken because Jiang Qing, Mao's wife, had declared the piano a product of "bourgeois liberalism."

In his monologue "Swimming to Cambodia," Spalding Gray speculates that there may be a hidden cloud of evil that circles the earth and lights from time to time nurturing a fecund harvest of horror. Like Cambodia in the seventies, like Nazi Germany. If so, it had surely descended on China between 1966 and 1977. And it had not missed Xi'an, where the temples, the mosques, the museums, along with God knows how many lives, were ransacked and mutilated.

But this woman was cheerful, talking with pride about how they had reopened the church in 1980 after the "troubled times," as she put it.

"Now many people come. Over five hundred to each service."

"Today there are four services," her husband explained. "Two in the morning, two in the evening." He smiled shyly. "We would like to come to more than one but it would not be fair to take the space for other people."

I asked if many young people came to church.

The woman laughed, shaking her head. I said it was the same in America.

"Too busy," she sighed. "But later, I think they will. That is why it is so important for us to keep this church alive. Later our children may need it."

"Where do you go in China?" the husband asked.

"Kashgar." They look puzzled. I repeated it several times trying on different pronunciations.

"It's out west," I explained, "not far from the Afghanistan border." They nodded but it was clear they didn't know what I was talking about. Since arriving in China, I was yet to find anyone who knew where Kashgar was. Most people had never heard of it, and the ones who had, even educated ones like the couple in the church, considered it a part of another, distant country.

Yu Xu Ling appeared at my door the next morning at 8:00 A.M. He wore the same outfit of gray fedora, modish coat, and scarf.

We walked to the building housing the dining room of the Renmin, about a quarter of a mile walk circumnavigating one of the jutting wings of the Renmin mothership. It was cold and gray, the way it had been since we stepped off the train in Xi'an. The night before I'd slept badly and found it difficult to be cheered looking ahead to a morning of Christian fellowship and English lessons.

The Renmin dining room was on the second floor of a strange round building. A handpainted sign at the foot of the stairs proclaimed WESTEN DINNER ROOM with an arrow pointing upward. I never could figure out why they called it a Western dining room, except perhaps because the menu did offer a "hambergler." When we first saw it, David had wondered if it was something to eat or to arrest.

The dining room copied the Italianate theme of the park outside the hotel. It was a big room with a vaulted ceiling, columns, and sufficient peeling paint and dirt to give it the authentic feel of an abandoned palazzo. Because of the high ceiling (and the lack of heat), it was a terrifically cold place, consistently five or ten degrees below the temperature outside.

The food was awful.

Yu Xu Ling began with an explanation of who he was and what he did. It was a formal little speech of the sort

Mark had suggested I prepare for our ski brethren in Beijing.

He was a school teacher. He taught fifteen and sixteen year olds electrical engineering. "My life is church," he said. Then Ling handed me a collection of postcards and letters written in English.

"To whom it may concern," started one. "We recently had the pleasure of making the acquaintance of a Mr. Ling while visiting in Xi'an, China. He was very helpful to us, assisting us in enjoying his fine city. He speaks very good English. We can honestly say that it was one of the highlights of our trip to Xi'an making the acquaintance of Mr. Ling. Sincerely, Hector and Joan Rice, Houston, Texas."

Most had the oddly stilted phrasing of an English student intent on learning a second or third language. But they were authentic with postmarks from Houston and Minneapolis and Los Angeles. Two were written by Swedish female students. "Skol!, Mr. Ling! Come visit soon!" ended one.

The letters were carefully unfolded from a small bible Yu Xu Ling carried in his overcoat inner pocket.

"To America, if I come, how much money should I have?"

I didn't understand what he meant.

He bent low to sip from his coffee cup, which he held in two hands but did not lift from the table. He had not taken off his hat or coat. (Neither had I.) Peering upward, his tired eyes looked confused.

"To America, if I come, how much money should I have?" he repeated.

"You mean to live while in America?"

He nodded, smiling more happily.

"How long would you stay?"

"How much money would I need?"

I shrugged and tried to smile. Across the room I saw a Canadian I'd met the day before wearing the sort of felt-lined winter boots I wished I'd brought. I thought about trying to buy them from the Canadian.

"How much?"

It was a question I didn't want to answer. China was such a fantastically cheap place and salaries so low—his I was sure was under $120.00 a month—that whatever amount I suggested would have to seem like a fortune to Yu Xu Ling. This idea of coming to America, like the scraps of paper tucked in his bible, seemed to be holding him together.

"You would like to stay as long as possible?" I asked after a moment or two.

He nodded.

I tried to explain that it was very hard to say how much money would be needed, that prices and cost of travel varied enormously depending on where you went, by what sort of transportation, what you did . . .

"I do not need much. I do not need to eat much. I think maybe in five or six years I could get passport to travel. I have friends in America." He carefully fingered his collection of letters. "We are brothers in Christ." He looked at me, tilting his head. "Please, tell me," he whispered, his eyes darting around the room. "I can save money but how much? How much?"

Chapter Eight

L eaving Xi'an is not an easy thing to do. Fleming and Maillart reluctantly hitched rides with a convoy of trucks that "did not look as if they would leave the next day; they did not look as if they would ever move again." This proved to be painfully close to the truth.

For us it should have been easy. All we had to do was buy a train ticket to Xinning, pack our bags, and leave.

No, no, no.

The CITS office will sell train sleeper tickets to foreigners—but only three or more days in advance. This would make sense if it were a matter of reserving space, needing to contact another city to verify availability, any of those sorts of logical processes. What happens in practice, however, is that you request your ticket properly ahead of your departure date, and then on the day you are scheduled to leave, a member of the CITS staff bicycles over to the train station and tries to buy a ticket.

But no matter. There is no need to go through CITS. Anyone can do the same thing—bicycle over to the train station and buy a sleeper ticket.

At least that's the theory.

Let me describe the Xi'an train station. There is a main building of crumbling brick facing a typically massive dirt courtyard laced with broken glass and bits of masonry, generally the sort of effect induced by a moderate artillery bombardment. Since this courtyard is always jammed with people moving at panic speed—the only time Chinese seem to be in a hurry is at train stations and then they are *always* in a hurry—the dust kicked up is extreme.

Encircling the courtyard and station building is a stone wall about eight feet high strung with barbed wire. Whether this wall is intended to keep people out or in, I can't say. The gates in this wall are cleverly concealed on either side. Just finding them for the first time takes a good half-hour of questioning and hunting.

Inside the station, the scene resembles the World Cup soccer riot a few years ago in Belgium, the one the British press headlined KILLER PANIC. At waist height, the walls are riddled with windows slightly bigger than those on a largish birdhouse. These are the ticket windows.

Each window sells tickets only for certain precise and limited circumstances—such as non-express trains leaving on Mondays for Xinning. Another window will handle tickets for Tuesday. Another entire series of windows exists for express trains. And overnight trains. None of these are marked or arranged in order. To discover the designated purpose of each window, one waits in line. And waits and waits.

But the ticket windows inside the station are only part of the story. Sprinkled at random outside the station, some even outside the walls, are more ticket windows, each with a specific function.

There is nothing more complicated than buying a soft-sleeper berth. The reason for this is that soft-sleeper compartments are the most expensive and there seems to be a prevalent opinion in China that the more money you spend the more difficult everything should be.

To buy a soft-sleeper berth you must first find the window that exists for no other purpose than selling soft-sleeper tickets to foreigners. Since there are no other for-eigners around and any non-foreigner, i.e. Chinese, has never needed such a ticket window, finding this exact window takes hours.

In fact, the proper window is *behind* the train station, an utterly ingenious location as it is invariably the last place one would look. Be warned it is only open two hours a day. But when it is open and you lean down to fit your face directly over the tiny window and explain, trying not to cough as the attendant blows smoke at you, what it is you want, the attendant, taking a while to transfer a particularly persistent hunk of mucous from his lungs to your feet, will issue you a little piece of colored tissue paper. This is cause for great celebration until you realize it is not actually a ticket. This flimsy bit of tissue merely verifies the fact that you are a real foreigner. That's all. Trying not to think why this might ever have been in question, you must proceed with your little toilet paper scrap to the actual ticket window.

If you can find it.

The afternoon of our scheduled departure from Xi'an, Fran was felled by a mysterious fever and chills. David thought it was the chemicals and coal smoke of Xi'an. Our first day in town he had gone for a long run, returned absolutely glowing, then fainted.

"If I'd known China was going to be like this, I'd have acclimated myself by spending some time running behind diesel trucks," he said.

There was talk of staying in Xi'an for a few more days so that Fran could recover, but she insisted we leave that night. We had this conversation while she was lying back in bed and the three of us were gathered around her looking concerned. If painted, the scene would be titled "Death Bed Vigil In Chinese Hotel."

"If we don't leave tonight, we'd have to get more tickets," she reminded us. Her words hung in the room while each of us contemplated this terrifying possibility.

That ended all discussion.

Gear packed and loaded, we took a cab over to the Xi'an Restaurant. We had heard it seated over a thousand people and so naturally had avoided it.

It was a cinder-block building that looked like most of the better restaurants in China. There was no door, but a thick curtain, like a horse blanket, hung in front of the open doorway; snow whipped into the foyer that was lined with benches on each side crowded with people waiting to eat. Everyone was huddled into long, green People Liberation Army greatcoats. Beyond the foyer the restaurant was jammed, every chair filled and behind each chair stood a would-be diner, hovering, ready to grab the chair as soon as the current occupant was finished. The more aggressive types cruised around the room trying to spot the fast eaters.

The floor was concrete, littered with a mix of fish bones, chicken bones, cigarette butts, and spit. It was maybe a few degrees warmer in the room than outside. Everyone kept their PLA coats on while eating. Dark green paint covered the bottom third of the walls; the upper portions were a dirty white.

"This looks good," Mark said, reading the large menu shellacked to the wall in the foyer. A friendly-looking older waitress smiled and dispatched us to the fourth floor, the reserved space for honored guests. We made the climb in silence.

A table of drunk, rowdy party cadres were feasting in the top-level dining room. Two Swedes cowered at a nearby table.

"Stuart, if you start asking these people how many grandmothers they buried in the Red Guard, I think I'll be sick right here on the floor," Mark declared flatly. He had not been feeling well either.

It is a Chinese custom to order lots of beer at the beginning of a meal and stack up the cans on the table, working through them as the meal progresses. This is a habit evolved—I figure—through living with shortages. If beer was available, better to grab it quick before somebody else did. It also served as a public display of both wealth and drinking prowess. By the looks of it, the table of cadres was doing well on both scores.

Inexplicably, the place seemed to be partially heated. We stripped off the heavy coats we'd worn at every meal; that left me with only thick long underwear, a wool shirt, some high-tech Patagonia sweater-like thing, and a down vest. David and Mark both wore the green Chinese army hats with jutting flaps lined with suspicious black fur. In honor of the heat wave, they folded the flaps up. It gave them a winged, pterodactyl look.

The food was wonderful: sweet and sour pork meatballs, curried beef, chicken with bamboo and mushrooms. None of us felt very hungry, but we ate everything and ordered more. We ate an amazing amount.

Afterward, driving to the train station I had that rare sense of being very glad to be doing exactly what I was doing.

Chapter Nine

"**Y**ou don't want to go to Golmud. BELIEVE ME, you do not want to go there."

"Why?"

"It is the most ghastly place I have ever been. The most ghastly."

Normally I am quick to dismiss other travelers' opinions, never believing plebiscites were necessary to ratify itineraries. But in this case, the source did merit some respect.

Steve Johnson was a twenty-seven-year-old English computer programmer who had made a bundle working for Citicorp in New York City. Bundle in hand, he had left New York to do "a bit of traveling."

That was two years ago.

"Two years? You've been on the road for two years?" To Mark, whose announcement that he didn't like to travel was looking less and less like a bluff, this was tragic news.

"Well, it's not like I've been constantly in motion for two years, mind you. I've done the whole thing quite slowly."

"Yes."

"Stopped off in Thailand for a while; Burma, Malaysia, Sri Lanka—recovered from hepatitis there . . ."

"You've been all those places and Golmud is really the most . . ."

"Awful. Absolutely. I was there a few months ago."

"Can I ask why you're going back?"

"We're going to Tibet!" This was Nicki. She was a five-foot-tall Australian punk rocker who had attached herself to Steve and Melinda, Steve's American girlfriend. Nicki was pretty, with a black shock of hair that stood straight up and a declamatory way of speaking that made every sentence sound like an imperative announcement of glorious news. "I'm Nicki! This is Steve! We've been on the train for three days!"

Nicki, who was one of those people who disavowed having a last name—"Just Nicki!"—was eighteen years old. "I just told me mum when I finish my nurse's course that's it! I'm off!"

"What does going to Golmud have to do with getting to Tibet?" David asked.

"We're taking a bus!"

There was a bus, they explained, that left from Golmud every week for Lasha, a forty-eight-hour trip. "Everyone says it's just terribly uncomfortable!"

Nicki was riding soft sleeper with us to Xinning; Steve and Melinda were in hard sleeper. They had all wanted to travel hard sleeper but there were only two places available so Nicki, the odd woman out, moved up to soft. "Mind you, we could have all gone hard seat together," Steve said, "but we just rode up from Hong Kong hard seat and it really was a bit much."

"You rode hard seat—not sleeper—from Hong Kong to Xi'an?" I asked.

"Only three days. Really not so bad but you do get a bit stiff after sitting up the second night."

Steve had the sort of off-hand way of downplaying discomfort that was carefully aimed to impress. It was terrifically annoying but I had seen hard seat and I *was* impressed.

"It was terr-i-ble!" Nicki cooed from the top bunk of her four-berth compartment. She was wrapped in a huge PLA coat with long underwear underneath. It must have been Australian long underwear as its largely transparent qualities, clearly the product of a beach culture, raised serious doubts about its warming ability. Her three male bunkmates, all Chinese, did not seem to mind that her exuberant voice dominated the compartment. They hovered about her proffering cigarettes. Nicki, when she wasn't talking, read *The Female Eunuch*.

It was 9:00 A.M. but the sun was just beginning to rise. All China operates on Beijing time, so that even though we were a couple of thousand miles west of the capital, at least two or three time zones in a normal world, everyone here was getting up and going to work the same time as the people in Beijing.

I enjoyed this wackiness right away. Dawn is a time of day I have always liked but the problem, naturally, is that it comes too early in the morning. But thanks to the Chinese, sunrise was now rearranged at a much more convenient time of day—about 9:30 where we were, somewhere between Xi'an and Xinning.

If properly promoted, I figured this late dawn could be a much greater tourist draw than the ruined temples and defaced art work CITS tries to pawn off as MUST SEES. Special Sunrise Tours could be the next big thing in this part of the world.

If I had understood the conductors correctly, we were to arrive in Lanchow within the hour. It was the major city between Xi'an and Xinning. It had taken Fleming and Maillart eight terrible days bouncing on the back of a lorry—all the while "a woman was sick with extraordinary persistence," Fleming dryly noted—to reach Lanchow. Once there, they were placed under open arrest, delayed for days, and eventually told they could continue but their Russian guides and, by now, good friends, the Smigunovs, could not. Lanchow was not their favorite place.

But if there was a major city just down the rail line, the landscape gave no clue of it. We were running through a stark, impressive piece of the earth. Deep ravines jutted into terraced hills dusted with snow. Thin frozen streams flashed in the gullies. Birds swirled across a sky hurrying from late dawn haze into a piercing blue.

Every few miles there was a cluster of houses, each formed of brown mud capped with a straw roof. No structure, even the most crumbling, lacked a high mud wall surrounding it. As defense, most of the walls would have done a poor job: they were gapped and broken in spots, with large ungated entrances. But they divided the long vistas down into a manageable scale and helped to carve out chunks of living space in the harsh land.

A freight train flashed by carrying army trucks on flat bed cars. When the last car cleared, we found ourselves in front of a large commune. It was, I was learning, a typical sight in China: in the middle of nowhere would appear a pair of twin smokestacks and a walled, ten-acre compound, displaying a big red star on its iron gate. It would be a tiny plant making gun parts or tractor transmissions, staffed invariably by Han Chinese sent from another part of the country, some as punishment for ideological impurity, say in the anti-rightest campaign of the late fifties, others according to the arbitrary whims of a Beijing bureaucrat. FERVENTLY PURSUE THE STRUGGLE FOR GREATER PRODUCTION read the slogan over the commune's gate. There was always a slogan.

At 10:30 we rumbled through Lanchow. Though Fleming and Maillart had a rough time there, Lanchow in those days sounded like a pleasant city.

> The streets of Lanchow are romantic. . . .
> There is a bazaar much nearer in atmosphere to
> the bazaars of Central Asia than to the markets
> of Peking. It is all very different from the China
> you see from the Treaty Ports; you have the
> feeling that you are on the frontiers of another
> land, that you have come almost to the edge of
> China.

But since 1935 when Fleming was here, the Beijing government had been at work bringing its own special brand of modernity to the place. Not so very long ago, this had been the edge of China, at least Han China, but such cultural anomalies had faded. Now there were the same dirty, pockmarked housing blocks that we'd seen everywhere, the ones that looked like medium-rise condos after a brisk mortar attack. The scene through the train window was a nightmare of industrial revolution England: scores of smokestacks belching in the background while steam engines shunted back and forth and half-nude children played on slag heaps of coal.

"Tell me, if a small group of Americans wanted to paralyze a medium-sized city in China, how would they go about it? I mean, purely theoretically, of course."

David was talking in the corridor with a large fellow in a uniform I'd never seen, sort of half-Army, half-train conductor. He spoke a little English. I wondered how much.

"We were particularly interested in any nuclear power plants you might know of."

David's friend listened intently, scrunching his eyebrows together in concentration. Mark buried his face in Stephen King's *It*. Fran also hid behind a book. But she was laughing.

This was not the first time that David had politely

inquired about the possibilities of terrorist targets. It was a gambit that began to develop on the train to Xi'an when we were talking with the train engineer. The topic had shifted to Chernobyl, and David had asked a number of sensible questions about the state of nuclear power in China. Later, I'd kidded him about how his interest might be misunderstood. It was Fran, I think, who suggested that next time David just get right to the point. "If a small group of Americans wanted to paralyze a medium-sized city in China, how would they go about it?" This became a question we tended to pose in lieu of more standard tourist questions such as, "What dynasty was this built in?" Even Mark liked it in a way, as it steered the conversation away from my regular inquiries along the lines of grandmothers, graves, and the Cultural Revolution.

The man in the uniform didn't seem to have an answer for David but he wanted to make friends. Moving into our compartment, he crowded onto the bottom bunk. He asked if we knew "fighter, Ali?" This was accompanied by a vigorous demonstration of Muhammad Ali's style. Our new acquaintance was a big man, and the compartment did not really give him enough room to do Ali's style justice. But he tried very hard.

Mark gave up on Stephen King. He started talking with our visitor in Chinese. What sort of uniform was he wearing? I posed the question through Mark.

"He's sort of a customs official," Mark explained after a lengthy exchange. "It's his job to check out anyone traveling west who seems suspicious."

"Oh," David said.

The boxing fan, who had spent his entire working life on the train, was a movable security guard assigned to the Xi'an to Xinning route. His wife lived in Ürümqi where he was born, a two-day train ride north. They saw each other only a few times a year.

He did not hesitate to talk about why the Xi'an to Xinning route required security officials like himself. Xinning was in the eastern edge of Qinghai province; there were prison camps in Qinghai province, many of them. It was important to know who was traveling in and out.

As we rumbled west, the towns grew smaller and the train yards larger. At one of the towns that seemed to be all rail yard, I got off to get something to eat from one of the old women pushing wooden food carts. Hideous, red shriveled chickens—chickens that looked like the aftermath of radiation experiments—were the popular item of the day. Dubiously I bought one of the tortured beasts for eight kuai along with two packages of crackers wrapped in brown butcher paper.

Back in the compartment, everyone stared at the chicken in amazed disgust. I ventured a bite. It tasted like the wrapping paper looked. I put the chicken down on the bunk where it sat the rest of the trip, taking on a certain quality not unlike a conceptual art piece. We ate the crackers. They were delicious. Jumping off to get some more, I was halfway across the dirt platform when the train started moving. I had a sudden, terrifying vision of being stuck in this town with nothing to eat but radiated chickens. A few feet away the toothless peddler waved one of her chickens, beckoning coquettishly. I scrambled frantically back to the train, breathing the sour bathroom smell that permeated the car with fond relief.

When we got to Xinning, I was still hungry. We left the chicken on the bunk.

Chapter
Ten

X inning opened as a disaster. It was Mark's birthday, something he confessed on the train with a groan, looking out at a particularly bleak stretch of landscape. "It's my birthday . . . ," he said in a tone that implied he wasn't at all sure he expected—or really wanted—to have another. Most definitely not if it had to be spent in a dark brown landscape where a Mongolian pony pulling a metal canister of human excrement was an event.

So Mark, we decided, was going to have a blow-out birthday, and if we couldn't deliver his girlfriend, whose Polaroid photos he examined with increasing frequency, then at least we could make him forget that he was in a part of China especially well-suited for the detention of criminals.

We decided to get the best rooms at the best hotel. Steve and Melinda, who had been here within the last year, told us that there were two choices—one was seven yuan a night ($2.20) and then there was the posher place at nine yuan.

"What the hell, let's go for broke," David asserted. "Nine yuan be damned, it's Mark's birthday."

The Xinning Binguan (Binguan means "hotel") is a sprawling, ugly building that was built by the Russians as a conference center. Like everything else in Xinning, it is dark brown.

We arrived there jammed into the back of a tiny

three-wheeled "truck" that looked like a rider-lawn mower with a cab. Half-asphyxiated from the exhaust fumes, we fell into the lobby. The first truly dangerous-looking men I'd seen since leaving my neighborhood in New York were lounging on a couch. They were brown-skinned Nepalese, with long stringy black hair and maybe a half-dozen teeth between them. Had someone informed me that they were assassins provided by the hotel as a service, like bellhops, I certainly would have believed it.

"What we want here," I told Mark, "are the rooms this place would give Deng Xiaoping if he were in town. "Number one, primo, right?" Mark was looking a little happier.

We ended up in a pair of two-room suites. The walls, like the hallways, were painted in a style popular with sanatoriums and reform schools: a gangrenous band extended upward from the floor about four feet, topped with a white so dirty it was moving toward gray. Once at a ski training camp I wore the same white T-shirt every day for a month without washing it, and just before it fell apart, the color was the same deeply textured grime as these walls.

The beds were stuffed with some kind of animal hair; we tried to guess the exact species by the odor wafting upward. David bet on improperly cured horse hair, while Fran insisted it was dog. The bathroom appeared to have a dirt floor.

"This is fantastic," Fran said, and we all agreed. After the cramped train compartment, we thought we had stumbled onto the Ponderosa.

The agenda was a hot bath and then a lavish celebratory dinner.

"There's something wrong with this water," Fran announced, peering into the tub.

"Like what?" David asked. He was not one to tolerate squeamishness in trivial matters like rusty bath water.

"There isn't any."

"Oh," I said.

"There's got to be cold water," David asserted. The differences between hot and cold baths seemed purely pedantic to David.

"Nope. Nothing. Strictly Sahara."

David flushed the toilet. Nothing happened. No water, no toilet. Now each of us had done quite nicely without toilets before, but usually the absence of toilets was accompanied by a certain proximity to the Great Outdoors. It's one thing not to have a toilet in the woods, it's another not to have one five flights up in a Russian Conference Center in the middle of China.

"I'll ask the front desk," I said, lifting a massive black telephone that had probably been installed in the room specifically for Deng Xiaoping. In the distance, like the sounds from a conch shell, I could faintly detect a voice. "Wei! Wei!"

"Let's just go down to the desk and ask," I said with the sort of phony good cheer no one believed. "I'm sure we can get it fixed or move rooms or something."

We walked down the half-mile long dark corridor to the stairs. There was an elevator but it appeared to be a ceremonial item reserved for special rituals. On each floor by the wide granite stairwell there was an attendant's desk. The attendants—or Fu Yen in Chinese—were very important individuals. Not only did they hold the key to every room—no keys were given out—they also were the titular leaders of the Cleaning Brigade. (This is their phrase, I assure you.) The Cleaning Brigade was important not because Brigade members cleaned—no one seemed to go in for that very much—but because they were also in charge of towels and the twice-daily thermos of hot water.

The latter were critical survival items. China is a country in which not even the natives drink the water unless it has been boiled. What stands between you and death by dehydration (or alcoholism, beer being the only other easy alternative) are thermoses of hot water that magically appear everywhere.

Walking down the stairs to the front desk, David and I debated whether we should call in Mark to translate.

"Didn't somebody at the desk speak a little English?" David asked. "It'd be better if we could handle it ourselves." David had grown quite fond of Mark and was eager to spare him any unpleasantness.

"Let's try," I agreed.

The scene behind the hotel desk was typical—a half-dozen people drinking tea and talking agitatedly. I had always heard how hard everyone worked in China, but I was yet to encounter a situation where there weren't five or six people assigned to do what one person could easily accomplish. The total impression this created was one of institutionalized lethargy. In some countries, of course, particularly those of a southern clime, this is accepted as the national character. But in a nation that was organized from cradle to grave according to a structure of work units, where everyone wore worker numbers, in which operas have been performed with titles like "Hail the Return of The Manure Gatherers," this endemic torpor came as a shock.

Out of the large pool of desk staff, we found a woman in her early twenties who spoke a little English. She was smiling and helpful.

She explained the water would be turned on after 8:00 P.M. It was off every day between 11:00 A.M. and 8:00 P.M.

Thus reassured, we headed for dinner.

We'd invited Steve, Melinda, and Nicki to join us.

The dining room looked splendid: a cavernous place with high ceilings, clean tablecloths of a nonplastic variety, even chandeliers. A formal black velvet sign above the entrance announced THE SECOND DINING ROOM.

Seated around the round table with a rotating center pedestal—what I grew up calling "a lazy Susan"—we toasted Mark with Chinese champagne. The waitress, not an especially friendly sort, told us there was one set menu, three kuai each payable in advance. David and I insisted this was our treat and ponied up the 75 cents per head. The idea of taking six people to dinner for under $6.00 appealed to us both. Moving from the dubious champagne to the always dependable Five Star beer, we awaited the feast.

It was awful. A swirling bowl of dirty water and greens, a pile of cold liver, some joints that not only Fran pegged as dog meat. The rice had grit in it.

Each of us made a feeble attempt to deny the obvious with a cheerful front.

"Gee, what's this?"

"This looks great!"

"Happy birthday, Mark!"

But we were all too tired to carry on the charade for long. A silence descended on the table.

Next to us, a group of cadres were downing platter after platter of decidedly different, delicious-looking food. We got Mark to ask our waitress if we could be served some of the food they were enjoying.

"She says it's not possible," Mark replied after the woman had barked at him.

"Why?" I asked.

"It's too late, she says. The cook has gone home."

Through the open kitchen doors I could see several very cooklike figures walking around.

We ate for a while more, each of us taking turns

trying to brighten the atmosphere. I finally left the table and headed for the downstairs desk. I had just asked to see the manager when Mark joined me. Knowing how much he hated any sort of confrontation, it was a significant show of good faith. Under Mark's gentle questioning, the desk clerk directed us to the kitchen at the rear of the FIRST DINING ROOM. We walked through a room even more lavish than the SECOND DINING ROOM past crowded tables of what appeared to be a conference of party leaders. They were all eating wonderful food.

It was a typical Chinese-styled confrontation. They—the kitchen manager and his assistant—trotted out a series of lies and we politely let them know we knew it just wasn't so.

The hotel has run out of food, they said.

But the room next door has enough food to feed all of us ten times over, we replied.

Yes, but unfortunately the cooks have gone home.

But there are five cooks right around the corner.

Yes, but it is too late for them to cook. You see regulations . . .

Finally we got down to money. They wanted more for better food.

I forked over an outrageous amount of money for a meal in China—about $35.00 or so. By comparing it with how much a good meal in New York costs, I accepted with alacrity the sudden seven-or eight-fold increase. Of course this same rationalization—cheap by New York restaurant standards—can be used to justify almost any extravagance, from vacations to high-performance sports cars. But it was Mark's birthday, by God, and I wanted to cheer him up. I was also quite seriously worried that I might be entering the first stages of anorexia.

After a vigorous round of extended handshakes and smiles, we headed upstairs to await our feast.

The new round of food was horrible. There was now a massive amount of inedible dishes piled up in the middle of the table. For the first time since arriving in China, I was angry.

It was all hopeless, of course. Even if the hotel had magically summoned the most exquisite food in China, it is doubtful the evening could have been saved. We had wanted to have a nice dinner for Mark, had tried, and failed. We got up to leave; all we wanted was a bath and bed and the chance to start over in the morning.

But there was still no water in the rooms. We should have guessed this by the horrific odor eminating from the bathrooms we passed in the hall. No wa wa, no flushee.

Now even Mark was annoyed. Tromping back down the five floors to the lobby, we caught the hotel manager as he was slinking past the Nepalese assassins toward the door. He was very sorry, he said, but he could not talk with us because he had an important meeting to attend.

At 9:30 at night?

The manager was a large man in his fifties with a dignified, almost elegant face; he seemed pained by a lie obvious even by Chinese standards.

We adjourned to his office. It was a musty, lifeless place like every office I'd entered in China. I was coming to think of these offices as Dead Zones, which emanated some mysterious rays curtailing all human exertion and activity.

Very deliberately, the manager took out a pad of paper and wrote at the top: A REPORT.

Then he explained to us: the pipes were broken. This was very unusual.

But we had been told that the water was off every day between 11:00 A.M. and 8:00 P.M.

"Yes, that is true. It should come on at any moment."

Fine, we said. We were certain he wouldn't mind waiting with us until it did.

No, no, no, the water was off for the entire city. No one had water.

But there was water in the kitchen. We had seen it. We must not know how to work a bath faucet.

This was, we assured him, a matter in which we had some experience.

It was only on the fifth floor that there was no water. The pressure was bad.

Each—shall we call them fictions?—was presented with increasing exasperation by the manager, whose name was Ma Tong. Mark seemed even more unhappy than the manager but he stuck with it, translating each response. By the time the water pressure story was offered, an explanation that we guessed was close to the truth, manager Ma had worked himself into a frenzy. He was sweating and talked in a loud voice, gesturing boldly.

Our exchange was reaching a crescendo as Ma, despite the loss of face, had started to offer us new rooms on lower floors (while still asserting intermittently that the water would come on, the pipes were broken, we didn't know how to work a faucet), when suddenly the entire hotel crashed into darkness.

We sat in the tight room in silence. Shrieks floated down the miles and miles of halls.

"Shit! Why tonight?" Ma moaned, as he fumbled for the phone and screamed, "Wei! Wei!"

Chapter
Eleven

"Life in these circumstances was an anxious, dragging, squalid business."

That's how Fleming felt when he was stuck in Xinning. It was an opinion he formed even without staying at the Xinning Binguan. What soured Fleming and Maillart on the town was the immediate discovery that Xinning looked to be about as far west as they would get.

> It was passport trouble again. In Lanchow the authorities, when they gave us back our papers, had assured us that they were in order for Chinghai [i.e., Qinghai province]. But they were not; before sending us on to Sining [Xinning], Lanchow should have provided us with a special passport. By failing to do so Lanchow had neatly delegated the responsibility for stopping us to her neighbors, while at the same time increasing both the likelihood and the legality of such action on their part; it was a beautifully Chinese gambit, in the best tradition of passive resistance. It looked as if we were done for.

That was fifty years ago but reading it in Xinning gave me a prickly sense of literary déjà vu. To follow Fleming and Maillart's trail, we needed to reach Golmud, then somehow travel northwest a couple hundred kilometers to the road that circled the Takla Makan desert and follow it to Kashgar.

We had absolutely no idea how to do this. There was a train to Golmud, and the word in Xinning was that foreigners could take it, but once in Golmud—that supposedly "ghastly" place—we knew we'd need permission to go any farther. My Bartholomew map showed one thin, squiggly road heading west from Golmud that appeared to be more or less the same route Fleming and Maillart traveled in '35. It ran through the far corner of Qinghai province into Xinjiang, dead-ending (a particularly apt phrase, I'm afraid) at another squiggly, even thinner red line that circled the Takla Makan desert.

Cartographers would tell you that the Takla Makan is part of the Gobi, sort of a southwest suburb of the largest desert on earth. But in practice everyone who had to deal with it one way or the other seemed to think of the Takla Makan as a separate world by itself, a massive, nasty place impossible to ignore.

"No traveler has a good word to say for the Taklamakan," wrote Peter Hopkirk in his book, *Foreign Devils on the Silk Road.* "Sven Hedin, one of the few Europeans to have crossed it, called it 'the worst and most dangerous desert in the world. Stein [a British explorer], who came to know it even better, considered the deserts of Arabia 'tame' by comparison. Sir Percy Sykes, the geographer, and onetime British Consul-General at Kashgar, called it a 'Land of Death,' while his sister Ella, herself a veteran desert traveler, described it as a 'a very abomination of desolation.' "

Like faint stars in rough orbit around a dying sun, oasis towns ringed the edge of the Takla Makan. The caravan route that linked the oasis had been utilized by traders since the first century B.C. Initially jade was the major commodity, carried east from Kashgar and Hotan to Lanchow and the markets of coastal China. In the third century, the direction was reversed, as China began exporting to the West the product that eventually lent its name to the trade route: silk. There was a northern and a southern route, each menacing. Caravans from Xi'an bound for India would veer northwest from Lanchow through the Gansu corridor to Dunhuang and then head either north toward Turpan and Korla or south through Hotan. Both routes ended—with luck—in Kashgar.

"In the spring of 1935, however," Fleming noted at the beginning of *News From Tartary*, "to have attempted to enter Sinkiang by either of these routes would have been most inadvisable." The problem was a simple one: war. It was a civil war with an international flavor. The Russians, Japanese, and Germans all had designs on Tartary with proxy armies of Moslem, Uighur, and Han factions fighting messy, indecisive battles over thousands of square miles.

To avoid these unpleasantries, Fleming and Maillart improvised. Here's how he explained their intentions before they embarked from Beijing:

> In the circumstances, the obvious thing to do was to find a route not generally recognized as such, and to take the province in the flank at a point where the influence of the provincial government—Soviet dominated and prudently exclusionist—might be expected to be weak. The map showed that our best, in fact our only chance of doing this was to go to Lanchow and thence—instead of following the Imperial Highway north-west to Hami, where we should have been either arrested, sent back, or got rid of in some even more humiliating and

final way—to continue due west across (not to be technical) the top right-hand corner of the Tibetan plateau. This route would take us through the remoter and not more than nominally Chinese parts of the Province of Chinghai, through the mountains round the lake called Koko Nor and across the basin of the Tasdim marsh, 9,000 feet above sea-level, until we reached the eastern ranges of the Kuen Lun. These, if our prospects were locally considered good, we should by some means cross, dropping down into one or other of the oases on the south of the Takla Makan, where we should find ourselves within Sinkiang and well on the main road to Kashgar.

Reading over this section in my room, smoking a two-cent cigar of suspicious local origin to ward off the smell of the erupting toilets down the hall, even Fleming's breezy prose made the whole thing sound ludicrously complicated. The thought of what it would take to explain the scheme to some bureaucrat made me want to run screaming down the endless, tunnellike corridors of the Xinning Binguan.

In the few days since Mark's birthday party, I had developed a fondness for the Xinning Binguan. Water and lights had returned to the hotel in irregular but adequate seizures, and I enjoyed the large rooms with windows overlooking the dusty square in front of the hotel. The square was lined with poplar trees, leafless and starkly pretty, and each morning, noon, and evening the square was filled with earnest Chinese hurrying to the FIRST DINING ROOM. These were the conference attendees. Though I asked a half-dozen people, I never got an answer I could understand as to what sort of conference was being held. Two people used the phrase "management technique" in their attempts at explanation, and I assumed they had been reading "I-coke-Ah." Everyone at the conference, male and female, wore a neat blue Mao suit; while outside, many favored the white surgical masks that the Chinese utilize as protection against the dust, cold, and pollution. From my window it made a strange sight: a scurrying mass of identically clothed, masked people moving in unison with one imperative.

I fell into a pattern of waking early and reading while listening to the Voice of America. The morning breakfast rush would pass under my window while I read Fleming, pondered about what we would do next, and drank coffee.

The coffee was very important. The more strange and outlandish our circumstances became, the more I enjoyed its familiarity. (Fleming himself, I rationalized, had depended on Worcestershire sauce for the same support. He carried a bottle with him from England.) With a certain ritualistic concentration, I mixed the instant I had lugged from Beijing with the hot water supplied in a thermos each morning by a member of the Cleaning Brigade.

I drank a lot of the coffee—all four of us did, actually —and we quickly learned that it did not take long to go through a single thermos of hot water. Unfortunately, despite my pantomime pleadings, the attendants held firm to the principle of one thermos only per room per A.M. and P.M.

After a few days, I took matters in my own hands and tracked down the source of the precious hot water. I did it by lurking in the shadows of the hall—an easy trick considering there was only one light every fifty yards or so—while one of the Cleaning Brigade distributed the morning's ration. This was done from a massive cart the attendant pushed: a slow, deliberate procedure, involving halting at each room to deliver a full thermos and bring out an empty. Logic dictated—and I had put a lot of thought into this—that when all the full thermoses had been unloaded, the emptys would have to be taken someplace to be refilled. If I could find that secret place, odds were I'd have a chance of an unlimited supply of hot water. This was a delicious thought.

After a long stalk, my quarry returned to its lair. (It says something, I suppose, about the state of mind China had put me in that I found spending a morning trailing a teenage girl with thermoses of hot water around a hotel an entirely worthwhile endeavor.) In a small room I discovered a device that looked like the top stage of a medium-sized rocket; a gleaming, cone-shaped cylinder with an impressive compliment of pipes swirling around the base. Scores of shattered thermoses lined the walls of the musty room. The space had an eerie feel to it, like the elephant burial grounds of the Great White Hunter movies I'd loved as a kid.

Walking back to my room, glowing with triumph and weighted down with booty, I ran into Mark.

"Guess where I've been?" he asked. He seemed unusually happy.

"Where?" There weren't many places to go in Xining.

"CITS."

"But you're smiling."

"I think I've arranged for us to get to Kashgar."

"On the Southern Silk Road?" We had started to call Fleming and Maillart's route this, though it wasn't entirely accurate.

He nodded, beaming. "I'll tell you all about it."

Fran and David were called to hear the news. The story went like this:

Mark had gone by the CITS office, though he didn't really expect anyone to be working because it was Sunday. (It is a typical Chinese contradiction that the only entity opposed to religion is the government, and the only workers who seem to consider Sunday a holiday are government office workers.)

"But I found these two guys inside," Mark explained, "watching television. So I go in and start talking about about how we're these Americans traveling in China and how much we love China and how we've always had this dream."

"Dream?" I said.

"I told them a relative of ours had made a journey many years ago across China and written this book about it and that we had always wanted to follow in his footsteps. Then I pull out my map and tell him what we really want to do is arrange a car to go by the southern route. And this old cadre starts talking about how difficult the roads are and how it's desert.

"So I say, you know, we're all from the American southwest and we love the desert. Our trip to China has been wonderful, but we really miss the desert and we would love to see the Chinese desert because we know it is the greatest in the world.

"They loved this, naturally. But they were still hesitant. So I told him how we had been saving for years to come to China and what a wonderful place it was and how special . . ."

Mark finally wore them down. They told him to come back tomorrow morning and everything would be arranged, no problem.

We celebrated with a fresh round of instant coffee.

The next morning Mark and I appeared at the CITS office at precisely 9:00 A.M. We were loaded down with

Marlboro cigarettes, which Mark assured me every Chinese loved. He had brought them from New York as extra-special wampum. The door was open but the room was empty. We took a seat.

The office was dark and cold. Posters on the wall celebrated Qinghai province as a vacation spot. They were written in Chinese and therefore, it seemed a fair assumption, intended for a Chinese clientele. I wondered how many countrymen were eager to visit the region of their nation primarily noted for its prison camps. Perhaps it was common; in America, after all, we had turned Alcatraz into a tourist mecca.

We waited an hour. The phone behind the counter rang constantly. Every few minutes someone would walk by the door, stop to look at Mark and me, and then walk on.

Finally we got up to wander the halls. There were many offices, all of them filled with people talking, drinking tea, and playing Tiao Qi, the star-shaped Chinese version of checkers. A few doors down from the CITS office, Mark stopped and said in a puzzled but excited voice, "That's him," gesturing inside the office.

"Who?"

"One of the guys I met yesterday at CITS."

"But—"

Mark entered and greeted the official with great charm. He was a fashionably dressed man in his mid-thirties with intelligent eyes. He seemed to be cut from the same young executive cloth as Pan Wei Men, the Ski Association chairman we had met in Beijing. His last name sounded like Kahn. We spoke in English.

Mark began by recapping our travel request, reiterating our love of the American southwest. Marlboros were offered. Kahn did not smoke. Mark gave an impassioned performance, closing with, "We know this is something we could only do with the help of CITS."

"Yes, you should talk with them."

Mark and I looked at each other.

"Aren't you with CITS?" I asked.

"No, no, I am head of the Transportation Brigade."

"But that's part of CITS, isn't it?"

He shook his head. "They are a separate work unit."

"But yesterday," I said, trying to sound as upbeat as Mark, "you were in the CITS office."

"Yes. Our television is broken."

"Oh."

We smiled at each other athletically.

"But if you want to get to Kashgar, you must have a car," he said after a while.

"Yes . . ."

"To get a car, you must get it from the Transportation work unit, not CITS."

"So you can help us?"

"Of course."

This was more like it. For the next hour we went over the route in detail. A four-wheel-drive vehicle would be needed, we all agreed, with extra gas tanks and an experienced driver. The price was high by Chinese standards but certainly less than it would have been in America. By measuring distances on the map, we figured the route was about 4,000 kilometers. We all shook hands on the deal. Mark and I were beaming.

"Of course I must get permission," Kahn said just as we are leaving.

"Permission?"

"From CITS."

"But I thought you were in charge of the transportation work unit."

He frowned. "I am, of course. But CITS is in charge of all foreign tourists. You are foreign tourists so they must approve."

"Will they say yes?"

"Of course."

"How long will it take?"

"Not long. A day or two."

"But we wanted to leave tomorrow."

"In a day, maybe two. No problem."

Naturally, this made us nervous. But Kahn's intelligence and apparent competence were reassuring.

During the short walk back to the hotel, we decided to spend some time tracking down traces of Fleming and Maillart on holy ground.

Chapter Twelve

On the ninth of September, 1951, the Chinese People's Liberation Army marched into the Tibetan capital of Lasha. At the time there were nearly four thousand monasteries in the country. By the end of the Cultural Revolution in 1976, thirteen monasteries remained.

Some 30 kilometers outside of Xinning, there is a monastery built in 1577 that is considered by Tibetans, particularly those of the Yellow Sect, to be one of the holiest in Tibet. But according to the Chinese government, the monastery is in China, not Tibet. In a nicely ironic touch, this annexation probably saved the monastery from the destruction of the last thirty years. It wasn't bombed or mortared by the army during the invasion of Tibet or subsequent rebellions, and when the Red Guards wanted to destroy all vestiges of Tibet's past—which is to say its culture—they concentrated on the Tibet of 1966, not its former territory.

While Fleming and Maillart were stuck in Xinning waiting for the verdict on their passport troubles, they were carted off—literally in a Peking pony cart—to the monastery of "Kumbum," some five hours from Xinning's south gate. No one we asked in Xinning had ever heard of Kumbum, but it seemed logical that it might be the same holy site the Chinese now call Ta'er Si.

We didn't take a Peking cart to Ta'er Si but I wish we had. We took a bus.

Chinese buses remind me of homemade bombs popular with counterinsurgents, the sort that are made by taking a metal can and packing it to the bursting point with every imaginable variety of nasty junk, from sharp metal objects to feces. I rode a lot of buses in China.

Just finding the bus to Ta'er Si took the better part of a morning. It does not, for some reason, leave from the bus station. This was explained to us after waiting in line for an hour at the station, a place so crowded, noisy, and dusty it made me remember the Beijing train station as an island of tranquility.

"He says only Tibetans take that bus, and we should ask a Tibetan where to find it," Mark shouted over the frenzy of a half-dozen people bidding for the attention of the Han ticket clerk.

In theory this advice was sound. There was no shortage of Tibetans in the bus station. We approached a family of five who stood in the middle of the station looking contentedly lost.

There was an old woman, a middle-aged woman, two very pretty teenage girls, and a young boy of perhaps twelve. All wore the standard yet fantastical Tibetan garb, the dominant item of which was a voluminous coat of roughly cured sheepskin tied at the waist with a bright scarf. The coat was draped off the shoulder, leaving one sleeve dangling empty and an arm, usually the right, unencumbered for sword play. The garments dragged the ground, as did the ends of the long scarves, but peeking out from beneath were thick, heelless boots that made the wearer appear burdened by club feet. Their hats were large bowls of brown fur, most probably rabbit, attached to a skullcap of brightly dyed cloth. With their brown faces jutting out from the encircling fur, the Tibetans looked at first glance like they had captured a wild animal and jammed it on to their heads.

"What's wrong?" I asked Mark after he had talked to them for a while.

"I'm trying to learn Tibetan."

"Oh."

The Tibetans, it seemed, did not speak Mandarin. Or Cantonese, of course, or any of the other odd dialogues Mark knew. Nor did they seem especially interested in communicating, at least not in a verbal way. What interested them was Fran.

In her black lycra stretch pants, red sweater, and aviator sunglasses, Fran was undoubtedly as exotic to the Tibetans as they were to her. She was also almost six feet tall. They circled her and stared.

Being stared at was something all of us, though especially Fran, had grown to accept. But the Tibetans stared in an unprecedented manner.

With a look combining the bliss and curiosity most commonly found in children, they placed their faces inches from Fran's. Heads slightly tilted, mouths open in more a smile than a gape, they stared.

There is something either lascivious or angry (or some combination thereof) about most staring. The Tibetans stared, though, with a passivity that was instantly endearing. They were curious so they looked. And they gave every impression of being able to continue this activity for many days to come.

The original group of five Tibetans soon grew to over twenty, all focusing on Fran. Eventually Mark was able to piece together directions of a vague sort. When we walked away, the Tibetans did not move; they watched us—or Fran—until we were hidden by the mayhem of pony carts and antique diesel buses that filled Xinning's main street.

* * *

The Ta'er Si bus left from a cinder-block shell of a building without doors or windows.

Behind the building, there was a dirt courtyard filled with antique buses, big things with bulbous snouts. All looked long abandoned. One of them was painfully filled with people, small animals, and large bundles. The roof rack held a layer of baggage and two or three more layers of humans. There were both Tibetans and Hans on the bus; the Tibetans looked happy.

A Chinese woman with an official look spoke to David.

Mark listened, scowling unpleasantly. "She says we should get on the bus."

"Which bus?"

He motioned toward the packed vehicle that conjured up images of a mobile ant hill; Fran was busy photographing this remarkable sight.

I thought of the scene in *News From Tartary* when Fleming and Maillart embarked on their first truck ride. "It had struck me as odd," Fleming wrote, "that a large crowd had gathered to see us off. I now realized that they were not seeing us off; they were coming too."

We looked at the bus in amazement. A week or two earlier we undoubtedly would have protested, but now we silently followed the commands of the woman motioning us on board.

Ten minutes later we lurched violently out of the courtyard.

With harsh cries and threatening gestures, the woman, who turned out to be the conductor, cleared some space for us.

Fran and I ended up riding the transmission hump; David was stuffed next to a Tibetan family, four adults and a baby shoe-horned onto a narrow bench. David was on the aisle, held in place by the crowd. Mark was part of that crowd.

Five minutes and maybe a half mile down the road, we stopped beside a small group of Tibetans and Hans. The bus doors opened.

"You've got to be kidding," said Fran, who had the best view.

Everyone on the bus—except for the Tibetans—started talking in loud voices. A dozen or so would-be passengers tried to press through the doors.

Mark had the worst of it. I caught a glimpse of him before he was ingested deeper toward the back; his Chinese army hat with fur ear-flaps was twisted down over his face. His arms flailed helplessly.

We stopped again shortly for another group. This time the driver pulled away with the doors still open. I couldn't see how many people were trapped half-in and half-out, but judging from the hoots of laughter, it made for a good show.

We stopped eleven times for additional passengers before we got to Ta'er Si two hours and 16 miles later.

The road twisted continuously upward, climbing into terraced brown hills dusted with snow. Ours was the only mechanized vehicle on the road. We passed carts pulled by donkeys, horses, yaks, oxen, bicycles, and people. At the sight of each cart—and there were many carts—the driver leaned on his horn. (Later, someone told me that Chinese law required a driver to honk when passing anything—man, machine, or beast; this may be a legal explanation for what otherwise would appear to be a national love affair with the horn.)

At one o'clock, bresting a low ridge, we saw below us the great monastery of Kumbum.

Its colored roofs, the tiles of one of them plated
with pure gold, crowded the steep slopes of a
narrow, sparsely wooded ravine; temples on
one side, low white-walled dormitories for the
lamas on the other. Figures in dark red robes,
diminished by the distance, threaded the narrow, climbing passages between the buildings.
A gong boomed lengthily.

That's what Fleming first saw at Kumbum. I saw a
basketball game.

Of course we weren't even sure that we were at
Kumbum. All we knew was that the bus was supposed to
go to a monastery called Ta'er Si and that monastery
might be the same one Fleming and Maillart visited.
When the bus finally shuddered to a stop, we happily
joined the crowd scrambling off. That our surroundings
did not resemble a monastery did not bother us at all. Any
change was welcome after the bus.

We were on a wide street, a mixture of dirt and
ruptured asphalt, in a small town. A basketball game was
in progress across the street in what was apparently a
donkey parking lot. The players were kids of about ten or
twelve, all Han Chinese; the tallest of the bunch held the
unattached hoop over his head.

Signs said that we were in Huangzhong and we
wondered if we had gotten on the wrong bus. The worst
part about thinking this was the idea that we would
have to take another bus back to Xinning and start all
over again.

Sloping upward, the main street was lined with stalls
selling merchandise of all description. Some were spe-
cialty stalls offering only footwear or sewing items while
others resembled miniature department stores with ev-

94

erything from needles and medicine to candy and knives. All the stands were run by Hans; Tibetans milled around them, mostly they just looked at the wares but occasionally one would reach deep inside his coat to come up with a bright blue or red leather pouch stuffed with tiny Chinese bills.

There was a rough, Wild West feel about the place. Donkeys and horses were tied to posts along the dirt streets; young Tibetan men carried daggers inside their waist sashes. It was cold but sunny in the thin, 9,000-foot air. Some of the Hans wore sunglasses, large-lens contraptions with gold braid on the side in a style favored by Libya's Colonel Qaddafi.

We found a restaurant, cinder block like all the other buildings, and entered through the heavy green blanket over the doorway. There were only five tables. In the kitchen at the back of the room, a Muslim cook and two female helpers worked with a giant skillet, not a wok, over a coal fire. Hunks of fatty lamb were stacked on a worn wooden table next to primeval-looking ribs and a mountain of onions. Everyone was very friendly.

We were served little bowls with three round nuts floating in a brown liquid. A large rock crystal rested on the bottom of the bowl along with an assortment of green leaves. It was tea, delicious tea sweetened with rock sugar and spiced with cinnamon balls.

Plates of mutton mixed with vegetables followed, then one giant platter of fried onions. It was all wonderful, an unexpected delight.

Curiously, a Caucasian woman sat across the room reading a book. She looked to be in her mid-sixties and wore classic European hiking garb—lederhosen, knee socks, and heavy boots. As we finished our onions, she walked over and asked, in a heavy German accent, if we had a corkscrew. David produced his Swiss army knife, and with it she opened a bottle of white Chinese wine.

By the time we left, many cups of sweet tea later, the woman had finished more than half of the bottle.

At a street stall, a Han selling music cassettes told us that the monastery was a mile past town. He was very excited by Fran's Walkman cassette player and offered her a tape of FAB FIFTIES FUN HITS if she would give it to him. The fifties designation was a loose one as the cassette featured four Chubby Checker hits and "Gloria" by the Shadows of Knight, a cover version of the Van Morrison song, all sixties' classics. When she refused his offer, the ante was upped to include an additional cassette of Negro spirituals. As we left, still declining the offer, he played "Let's Twist Again" very loudly as a final tantalizing lure.

As the road climbed toward the monastery, the goods in the stands shifted from practical items to more flashy offerings of the sort favored by Tibetans—silver jewelry, thick coats, boots, ornate daggers, and short swords. Young monks, bald and barefoot, in long robes of a soft orange tint, gathered to giggle and point to the weapons like schoolboys at a porn store.

The first thing you see as you approach Kumbum is a row of eight white chortens, which I believe commemorate eight lamas who were killed by the Chinese (perhaps during the Moslem rebellion of the '60s, when a lot of them were massacred and their temples partially sacked). We crossed a little bridge, passed the chortens, and turned left into the maze of buildings whose small trapezoid windows, wider at the top than at the bottom, seemed to frown down on us from under lowering brows.

Reaching the top of the hill that the monastery crowned and seeing the eight columns just as Fleming described, was the first time I had the pleasant, eerie feeling of truly following in his footsteps. Regardless of the name, we had definitely arrived at the right monastery.

There was great activity around the columns. Small groups of beautifully dressed Tibetans were striking dramatic poses. Several brandished vicious-looking swords, their blades glinting in the sun. I stopped and stared, trying to make sense of it.

Then I saw the photographers. Enterprising Han Chinese had set up photography booths complete with wardrobe departments. For ten yuan, the photographers equipped the Tibetans with outlandish leopard-skin robes, brilliant velvet sashes, massive fur hats, and gilt broadswords. Dressed in this finery, families posed dramatically in front of the columns while the Han photographers ducked behind the cloth backing of their old-fashioned box cameras mounted on tripods. Brothers posed together, arm in arm, and several very young male children were positioned by fathers in fearsome solo scenes, struggling with two hands to lift the long swords.

There was a country fair feeling in the air. Most of the Tibetans had come on a pilgrimage from the Lasha area, a brutal week-long trip by truck. It was for many a once in a lifetime journey—and a rare chance to see a temple and monastery not ravaged by the Hans.

In the weeks we had been in China, I had grown

accustomed to the monochromatic quality of Chinese life. To an extent difficult to comprehend, the Chinese have created a world void of variation. It is something that a visitor begins to take for granted, forgetting that there is an alternative. The eruption of lurid colors at the monastery was like a soft rain after a long drought.

The Ta'er Si monastery, as the Chinese now call it, was a collection of fantastically decorated buildings strewn over several miles of hillside. Religiously it served a dual function, providing temples for worship and a lamasery for the training of young monks.

> All around us lamas with shaven heads, in red robes or in yellow, paced and squatted in the courtyards. Others, inside the temples, seated rank upon rank in semi-darkness, endlessly intoned their prayers, sending up waves of rhythmic, hypnotizing sound to beat upon the scarlet pillars and the hangings between which a dull gleam betrayed the smiling and gigantic god. Here, in the greatest temple, looking down from a high gallery upon the huddled chanting figures, I caught for a moment, and for the first time, something of that dark and powerful glamour with which Western superstition endows the sacred places of the East. I had been, as every traveller has, in many kinds of temples; never before in one where I had that tight, chill, tingling feeling which I suppose is something between spiritual awe and physical fear.

There were moments in China, not many but a few, when I was struck not by how much things had changed since Fleming's day but how much they were the same. This was one.

We stayed at a small inn attached to the monastery. Each clean, square room had four beds and a small charcoal stove in the center. The rooms faced each other around a courtyard. All of the walls, inside and out, were constructed of bright orange, red, and green panels shaped into long rectangles and concentric squares within squares. The repetition of shapes made it difficult to tell where the doors were placed in the walls.

The other rooms were filled with Tibetan families, six and seven to a room. They huddled in the center of their rooms, their voluminous coats gathered up like gowns, talking softly; little children peeked out from the doors, waving hesitantly, looking like dwarves in their miniature fur coats.

On the way to the cement outhouse behind the inn, I ran into the woman who had borrowed the corkscrew at lunch. While we exchanged pleasantries, a team of earnest young women, masked and wearing tattered blue Mao suits, rolled a wheelbarrow up behind the toilets and began to shovel feces into it. All but the latest droppings were frozen, and they took turns hacking away with the edge of the shovel.

The woman was Swiss, from Sils Maria in the Engadine Valley. I told her I had been there many times and had raced in the Engadine Marathon.

"I travel everywhere alone," she said. "I think you see more that way." Her skin was brown and cracked. Standing, she listed to one side, as if one of her legs was shorter than the other. I wondered about a skiing accident, and the thoughts made me realize how much I missed the sport. A year ago at this time I had been in West Yellowstone, Montana, training for the season's first race.

"How long have you been in China?" I asked.

"We are not in China," she answered sharply then

laughed, though it sounded more like a bark. She peered at me, waiting for a response.

"The Chinese wouldn't agree."

"The Chinese." She laughed harshly. "Do you know how many monks were slaughtered in the Cultural Revolution?"

Slaughtered was a rough, un-Swiss word; I was startled.

"Do you see that?" She pointed toward the outhouse before I could answer. I started to wonder if she was crazy.

"The toilet?" It was far from a toilet but I didn't know what else to call it.

"Above, up. Look!" She gestured vigorously upward toward the side of a gaudy red temple beyond the outhouse. "Do you know what that says?"

Very faintly I could make out faded yellow Chinese characters near the top of the wall.

"No."

"Sayings of Chairman Mao," she pronounced. "The Red Guard. Even here. In God's world."

I nodded.

"Do you have extra?"

"I'm sorry?"

She pointed to the roll of toilet paper I was holding. "Tissues."

"Of course." I unwound a handful and gave them to her. She walked away to the side of the cement shack marked for women, separated from the men's side by a low wall.

On the way back to the inn, I rounded a corner and came upon a group of teenage monks playing soccer. The ball was made from a Tibetan fur hat stuffed with rags. The teenagers giggled as they bumped into each other, their long robes flowing behind them in the fading light of early evening.

* * *

The next morning I woke up early in the freezing room. Frost had formed on the inside of the window by my head. David and I went downstairs in the darkness to look for hot water for morning tea. We discovered a massive boiler in a small courtyard next to the inn. It looked like a blast furnace in a steel mill. A five-foot door was open and young Han women, perhaps the same women who had been at work on the feces detail, shoveled coal into the flames.

The orange glow of the flames played across a dozen or so Tibetans washing themselves in tin basins of hot water drawn from the boiler. Fran had joined the group. They watched her, fascinated by her toothbrush and washcloth and she watched them as they smoothly performed the seemingly difficult maneuver of washing without removing their long coats.

We had a breakfast of round white bread and rice mixed with egg. Before leaving, we talked with the kindly Han who ran the inn. He was old enough to remember Fleming, but he explained that he had been sent here from Beijing in 1957. He seemed surprised when we asked him about the name Kumbum. Only Tibetans used the name, he told us. Since 1957 he had learned to speak Tibetan. He liked it here, he said. He did not miss Beijing.

Walking back to the bus, Fran and I spotted a young Han wearing a huge pair of black fur mittens. The bristling fur made his hands look like transplants from a science fiction creature. "Wookie gloves," Fran called them. We bartered for the pair as a late birthday present for Mark. He seemed pleased.

On the way back to Xinning, I shared space on the transmission with a disagreeable monk who burped the entire trip, as if releasing air in adjustment to the declining altitude. When we reached the outskirts of Xinning, the driver, hand on horn as ever, plowed through a group of school children. They all wore the red kerchiefs of the Communist Youth League, and I could have sworn the bus clipped one but there was no cry from the street and the driver appeared unconcerned.

Chapter
Thirteen

We were back in the mighty Kahn's office at 9:00 A.M., and the word was go.

"No problem," Kahn said. He paused delicately. "You have money?"

What we had were traveler's checks, which we rushed back to the Binguan desk to exchange.

David was at the desk deep into conversation with a collection of attendants. They were questioning him about English idioms.

"It's not 'An itch in time saves nine,' it should be 'A stitch in time saves nine.' "

"I think it's 'A stitch in nine saves time,' " Fran suggested.

What about "Don't let the camel out of the bus?" they asked.

We talked about this for a long time. Finally David had a breakthrough. "You mean 'Don't let the cat out of the bag?' "

They nodded enthusiastically. "You tell us some more," they insisted.

"Catch 22," David said. "It is very popular."

He embarked on a lengthy explanation of its meaning.

"You mean how life is every day in China," a pretty female clerk finally said.

After the English lesson, we changed our traveler's

checks into a massive bankroll of Chinese currency and returned to clinch the deal with Kahn.

Reverting to Chinese, he explained there was a little problem. He did not look happy. The problems had something to do with the availability of gas and the conditions of the road. We explained that we had discussed all of this before and been assured that all these difficulties could be overcome. David pulled me aside and suggested I show Kahn our bankroll. With a gesture I remembered from riverboat gambler movies, I toyed with our wad of money in a calculated, nonchalant manner.

Kahn appeared completely unaffected. His embarrassment and frustration seemed genuine.

Come back at 3:00, he told us. He would definitely have an answer.

Back in the SECOND DINING ROOM we ate a dispirited lunch. I went back to my room, down the long, dark corridors, and fell into a dreamless sleep.

We returned to the office by 3:15. Kahn was not there. Cigarette smoke fogged the room. A fierce game of checkers was underway between two punks in dark glasses and high heel boots. One, who had a protruding sore like a tumor on his cheek, told us that the car couldn't be arranged, the trip was off. He did not look up from his game.

"There's nothing we can do," Mark said. He wanted to leave.

I refused. There was something about this passive acceptance—though it was clearly the logical choice—that made me want to do *anything* before giving up.

Searching the warren of offices on the ground floor, we found the young woman who was Kahn's assistant. The problem, she told us, was not the roads or gas. To get to Kashgar we had to leave Qinghai province and go through Xinjiang province.

We explained that we were aware of this.

Kahn's Transportation Brigade, she said, could not give us permission for any travel in Xinjiang province.

Mark told her that Kahn explained to us the first time we talked that he would have to get permission from CITS. But this morning he only mentioned problems with roads and gas so we assumed CITS had given him permission.

CITS in Xinning, she responded, could only give permission to travel in Qinghai province. They did not have any authority for travel in Xinjiang.

"Ask her why we weren't told this two days ago," I said. Mark had the pained expression he got when asked to translate something he didn't approve of.

"There's nothing she can do."

"Who *can* give us permission to travel in Xinjiang?"

An exchange followed in Chinese. "Only the Public Security Bureau," Mark translated.

"Does the Public Security Bureau in Xinning have the authority to grant permission to travel through a different province?"

She nodded enthusiastically.

"And if we had permission from Public Security, Kahn would rent us a vehicle?"

Again the answer was yes.

So we went to Public Security.

It was buried in the damp basement of an ugly building that must have been built by the Russians. The walls were dirty and shiny with moisture, and puddles dotted the floor.

There were three cadres in the office sitting at desks. They were all studying sheets of paper with photographs of individuals. The oldest of the three, perhaps fifty, had jutting buck teeth and seemed friendly. He wore round wire glasses with tiny lenses.

Mark started to detail our problem when another cadre, hunched over his papers, cut him off.

"Meo." He barked.

This meant "No, cannot be done." It was the one word in Chinese I had come to understand with dread clarity.

Mark started to say something else.

"Meo!"

Chinese yell at each other all the time. But this was the first time I'd heard anybody yell at a foreigner. There was a palpable meanness loose in the room like the moment in a bar just before the first punch is thrown.

David and I bristled. Mark looked at us plaintively. We left.

"You see," Mark said on the way back, "those are exactly the kind of guys you always find in Public Security Bureaus. They're holdovers from the Cultural Revolution, guys who got into power by making revolution, by yelling louder than everyone else. They hate foreigners. They especially hate Americans. For two years when I taught at Hunan I had to go to guys just like that for permission to do anything. There is nothing worse."

"Why don't we just forget about getting permission," I suggested. "Let's see if we can get some truck drivers to take us."

"I won't do anything in China that's illegal," Mark said. "I won't run the risk of getting caught and barred from ever coming back."

"But you hate China!"

"I know! But somehow my life's tied up with this place. I don't know how it happened but it did."

"But Mark, look, lots of people hitch rides with trucks. If you get stopped all they do is send you back to where you started."

"Not me! I'd be the first to get expelled. I know I would. Some asshole just like the asshole we saw five minutes ago in that basement would take me and personally kick me out. I know it!"

David said that if we didn't leave Xinning one way or another the next day he was going back to Beijing. "I can't take this waiting around. One more night in that hotel room and I've had it. I'd rather be in jail. I'm serious."

Kahn was in his office when we got back from the Public Security Bureau. We made a deal that we'd hire one of his four-wheel drive vehicles and a driver to take us to Golmud. All of the trip would be in Qinghai province, and Kahn assured us we wouldn't need approval from anyone else.

He introduced us to the driver. It was the punkish-looking fellow with the protruding sore. His name was Lou Shan.

When, after days of effort, Fleming finally managed to arrange transport out of Xi'an, he wrote in his diary, "We start at 8 tomorrow, I don't think."

I felt the same way about Xinning. But despite my doubts, Lou Shan arrived in front of the Binguan promptly at 9:00 A.M. The departure time was an item of some negotiation. David, who seemed serious about his need to get out of Xinning, argued for 7:00; Kahn thought 10:00 was pushing the necessary preparations. We compromised at 9:00.

Lou Shan drove a green four-wheel-drive Nissan van, an impressive machine of a newish vintage. We loaded the bags and then Lou Shan said casually that he had a few things to do before we left. There followed a period of gas gathering, headlight repair, and radiator filling, all the things Kahn had said needed to be done. In no way had Lou Shan let the 9:00 departure time affect when he intended to leave.

None of us really minded, though. We waited on the Binguan steps, dozing in the sun. Mark had been up all night with stomach trouble, and he stretched out on the concrete, moaning intermittently. Our suggestion that we wait another day before leaving made him moan louder.

Inside the Binguan in a cavernous conference room, French representatives of IBM were holding a demonstration. Lured by the heady thought of selling to one fourth of the world's population, foreign companies of all descriptions have descended on China. Turning up in the oddest corners, these sales reps are the new missionaries, hawking their goods and services with evangelical fervor.

When I dropped in on the demonstration, the entire staff of the first floor Cleaning Brigade was observing the Big Blue machines in respectful silence. I don't know if the sales reps understood the nature of the crowd they had drawn but they were putting on a very lively show.

In the bathroom down the hall from the conference room, one of the IBM sales staff stood with his hand on his hips looking distraught. He seemed very glad to see me.

"What's happened here?" he asked. He pronounced the sentence like Inspector Clouseau, "Vatt's happened vere?"

Like everyone who works for IBM, he wore a clean white shirt and dark tie.

"What do you mean?"

"Look. Each one." He opened the doors to each of the six toilet stalls, wagging his finger in alarm. The seats of the toilets were dotted with clumps of feces.

"It's that way every morning," I explained.

"What?"

I explained to him that many of the hotel's guests and staff preferred not to utilize the Western-style toilet in the accepted Western manner. They chose to squat on the toilet seat, as they did with the standard trench or hole-in-the-ground toilets.

"So?"

I wished he could draw his own conclusions. "It's a problem with aim," I finally said.

I left him there, staring.

We finally pulled away from the Binguan some time before noon, stopping at the post office on the way out of town. (No one had much faith in the postal services of Golmud and beyond.) It was an unusual building for Xinning, large and handsome with a European flavor. The ceilings were high, supported by columns that actually looked to be marble. Unaccountably, it was heated.

Five modern telephone call boxes lined the wall. All were filled with Hans. A Tibetan family sat on one of the benches in front of the boxes, as if waiting their turn. I wondered who they would be calling. The cries of WEI! WEI! penetrating the closed doors of the phone boxes drove me back outside.

About two miles out of Xinning, the paved road expired. Within four feet the surface shifted from smooth pavement to steep swells of gravel and dirt that stretched out endlessly like rough surf. Our heads bounced rhythmically against the roof of the van.

"This can't last long," I said. Mark looked as if he was going to throw up.

It lasted for several hours. In the middle of the road there were mounds of dirt piled at regular intervals. I have no idea what purpose they were intended to serve. It was the sort of thing a construction crew might have done but we passed no workmen or any other hints of road work. There were thousands of mounds.

It was entirely plausible the mounds were a mistake or a make-work job or both. Massive work projects seem to take on a life of their own in China. Outside Xi'an, we saw hundreds, perhaps thousands of trees each with a white band painted around it a few feet from the base. A driver explained to us that the trees were being sprayed with an anti-insect compound. This insecticide was intended to be sprayed on the lower fourth of the trees. So one crew of workers had marked a forest worth of trees with a white band indicating their estimate of each tree's lower fourth. Another crew was to follow to perform the actual spraying.

During the Cultural Revolution, all the beautiful ancient gates of Beijing city wall were destroyed. This was not random Red Guard violence but "the work of specialists, well-planned and well-organized, employing a large work force over many years until long after the end of the Cultural Revolution," writes Simon Leys in his study, *Chinese Shadows*. And yet no one seems to know why. "When cornered on the subject, authorities are vague and strangely laconic," Leys notes. "It is rather remarkable that nobody seems to know the true reasons for a job that took so much effort and so many people and lasted for so many years."

On the rough road from Xinning to Golmud, these strange mounds did not go unappreciated. Smiling truck drivers used them like the pylons of a slalom racing course, weaving their big diesels around the heaps with notable skill. Lou Shan, fortunately, did not go in for this sport. He had enough to contend with trying to avoid the swerving rigs carrying everything from yaks to anti-aircraft guns.

We, at least, had the mobility to avoid the vehicular onslaught. The pony and yak carts crowding the road made perfect targets. This did not seem to bother their drivers; most took a fatalistic approach, burying themselves deep under blankets to sleep away the long journey. It was a disconcerting sight: cart after cart plodding along with massive loads of hay or bulging sacks of onions without apparent human occupants.

For a long time we trailed a cabbage cart. Three children rode in the back, their coats pulled up over their heads. They looked like miniature Quasimodos.

The Huang Shui River ran alongside the road, thirty yards wide and laced with thick ice. Electrical wires of bare copper swung wildly in the wind, strung between rude poles.

In early afternoon we reached the first town, Huangyuan. In this jumble of concrete blockhouses, the road improved to a narrow strip of asphalt that felt like a four-lane highway. A double-row of poplar trees sprung up, providing the unexpected look of a French country lane.

Mountains dominated the horizon. Motor whining, the van climbed into a landscape of bleak rock and ice. At the end of a long series of switchbacks, two brilliantly colored pagodas sat on the crest of a ridge.

Lou Shan explained that these were watchtowers dating from the Tang Dynasty.

We stopped and climbed up to the structures. Mounted on slabs of concrete, they had the gaudy look of post-Cultural Revolution renovations. The view was extraordinary. In one direction, massive brown hills rumbled down toward Xinning; in the the other, flat grasslands stretched out to the horizon, bounded by mountains on both sides. It was a windy, exhilarating perch. The damp cell of the Public Security Bureau seemed very far away.

An hour later we reached the shores of Koko Nor.

Chapter Fourteen

In the years after I first read *News From Tartary*, it was the image of Koko Nor that I remembered most vividly. A vast salt lake, it appeared on maps of China as a splotch of blue on a brown canvas. In libraries or bookstores, I'd gaze at the map and wonder what this fantastic-sounding place was really like.

Koko Nor is the Muslim name. In Chinese, it is called Quinhi Lake, which means "blue sea" lake, the name that the Chinese have adopted for the province.

"The Koko Nor covers an area of 1630 square miles and lies over 10,000 feet above sea level," Fleming wrote. "The lake when we saw it was frozen. The glittering ice stretched, unbroken and unsullied as far as the eye could reach. It gave me a feeling of forgotten magnificence, of beauty wasted."

Fleming reached the lake in late March. In mid-December when we arrived, the sheets of ice extended from the shore, mixing with a residue of dried salt to give the impression of a giant glass lined with frost.

Before leaving Xinning, Lou Shan had loaded three jerricans of gas in the rear of the van. Poorly sealed, they sloshed gas at each bump, creating a minor toxic waste dump amongst our luggage. With salt water swooped from the icy edge of the lake and balsam shampoo from the Great Wall Sheraton, David and I washed the cans and tried to fix the seals with bits of rags. We worked in silence, shivering under the clear sky. Fran scrubbed a sleeping bag then draped it over the van to dry. Within a few minutes, it froze solid.

Koko Nor stretched out like the beginnings of a great ocean. The scene felt like the forgotten flood in a science fiction fantasy, the hidden sea in *Journey to the Center of the Earth*. Even the fish skeletons that washed in amidst the salt and ice looked unnaturally large and oddly shaped.

There was a large fish processing plant on the south shore of the lake and two bleak settlements, Jiangxigon and Hiemahe. In both, Han Chinese ran the few establishments, the one restaurant and the three or four outdoor stalls that were the only stores. Tibetan families drifted through town looking lost, neither happy nor distressed.

All the time we were in China, the only Tibetans I saw engaged in anything that might be considered work were sheep herders on the flat grasslands on the high plateau between Xinning and Golmud. By the time we reached Koko Nor, David had dropped his Indian comparison. The similarities between the Tibetans and reservation Indians of America were too obvious to note, too depressing to discuss.

A high pass rose at the end of Koko Nor. We drove through brown hills that looked more like sand dunes than mountains, peaks of dirt with sculpted surfaces of windswept ripples. The north slopes held pockets of dirty snow. It was lunar and disturbing, impossible to associate with anything that might be labeled Chinese. Looking back at Koko Nor, the sun glinting off the mounds of dirt and snow surrounding us, I felt we had finally left China to enter the edges of Asia.

*   *   *

That night we stopped outside a little town called Yanhu. Lou Shan drove through the main street of concrete and mud buildings to a large walled compound.

Twenty cinder-block rooms faced a courtyard on three sides. The courtyard was dirt, littered with broken glass, bits of coal, and shattered bricks. The doors to the room were reinforced with sheet metal. The one window in each room was laced with bars.

Lou Shan disappeared. We waited, shivering in the fading sun. Three young punks stopped to stare. They wore high-heeled shoes and talked in loud, drunken voices. I was frustrated and tired, depressed by this awful place. The prospects of a fight were appealing.

But the punks were friendly. "It's too late now," one said. "You should have been here in the summer. That's when it is nice here."

I tried to imagine what possible effect summer could have on this forsaken spot.

After half an hour, Lou Shan returned carrying three broken wooden planks. Three Han women accompanied him, pushing and pulling a large wheelbarrow of coal at a half-trot. Unexpectedly, they were young with pretty faces behind surgical masks dark with coal dust.

Lou Shan looked on smiling while the women opened two rooms and started fires in the coal stoves. A thick layer of dust covered everything. Lit by a single fluorescent light, each room had four coats and an armchair covered with tourist scenes of Qinghai province.

Outside the rooms, I picked up an empty can of Chinese meat and a bottle of Prince Shikakai Perfumed Hair Oil made in India. FOR LONG LOVELY AND LUSTRUOUS HAIR it read. SAVES THE HAIR FROM FALLING AND DANDRUF. There was a picture on the bottle of a buxom Indian woman with hair, long and lovely, extending to her feet.

Mark crawled into bed, moaning between shivers. In the stark room wearing his PLA hat with the flaps flying, he looked like a war photo of a dying soldier in a field hospital.

Our hotel, or perhaps more accurately, motel, was part of a compound of buildings that belonged to a work unit. Lou Shan shrugged when asked what sort of unit. Large red letters numbered each building. There was no grass, trees, bushes—the only visible living things were people and insects. Everywhere in the compound, the earth was hard-packed and littered with broken concrete.

Across the road another walled compound sat bleakly next to a railroad siding; a pair of smokestacks and a large cylinder structure like a grain elevator rose above the low walls. The smokestacks pumped black smoke into the sky, red with the setting sun.

We ate dinner alone in a large bare room. My thermometer read 36 degrees, despite the hot stove in the center of the room. The glass in all of the windows was broken; these windows were barred like the ones in our rooms. The food was good—omelets and stir-fried chicken with scallions. A plate of onions was served on the side. David and I talked about Jackson, Mississippi, about the neighborhood where I grew up and he used to live. I wanted to talk about Jackson.

At 2:00 A.M. that night I stepped out into the courtyard to piss. The sky was clear and luminous, the air urgently chilling. I thought about Fleming and Maillart crossing these frozen grasslands on foot and horseback. I was jealous. My body was sore from bouncing in the cramped van, but it wasn't the pleasing soreness of muscle exhaustion. Better to have spent the day walking and looking for a likely target for a little rook rifle.

Back inside, I stuffed the stove with coal and fell asleep.

At 6:30 I woke up shivering and fumbled with the stove. I tried to turn on the lights but the electricity was off. All electricity in China, except in Beijing, apparently died between the hours of midnight and 8:00 A.M. Half-asleep, an image came into my mind of a giant breaker switch in a tomb beneath the Forbidden City manned by one of the smiling girls of the Cleaning Brigade.

At breakfast two hours later it was still pitch black. Dawn was a mid-morning event this far west. While we ate warm mounds of chewy white bread, a shrunken-looking man came in with a load of coal for the stove. He was a Han and spoke Mandarin. With Mark reluctantly translating, we started to talk.

How long had he lived here?

Thirty years.

Why did he come?

I was sent.

Where did he live before?

Shanghai.

And his children, where did they live?

Here, he said. We all live together.

What was the industry across the road? The smoke-stacks by the railroad siding.

Salt. It's what we do here. Mine salt.

We finished breakfast in silence. I thought about Shanghai, thirty years ago the most cosmopolitan city in China, a tropical climate, beautiful buildings. He had most likely been sent here to—it was almost too stereo-typed—this salt mine in the anti-rightist campaign of the late fifties. Perhaps he was one of the flowers that had bloomed in Mao's Hundred Flowers experiment with plu-rality. One of the thousands—some said millions—who had followed Mao's lead and differed with the government only to be disciplined shortly thereafter by the Party. I wondered what he had thought when he arrived here and looked at the place where he and his children would spend their lives.

An omelet, cooked at our request, was delicious. We left Yanhu as the sun was coming up.

Chapter
Fifteen

I t's hard to spend much time in western China and not do a good bit of thinking about sheep. The animals appear everywhere, particularly at dinner time. Mutton is very big in western China.

Fortunately, I find sheep fairly likable creatures. And surprisingly interesting:

> The native sheep of China are of three main types: Mongolian, Tibetan, and Kazakh. The Mongolian and the Tibetan sheep differ in shape and size of tail and in coarseness of wool, the latter having the smaller tail and the longer, coarser wool. The Kazakh sheep is a fat-rumped breed.

I read over this section in my Chinese geography book on the main street of Dulun. I was surrounded by a couple of hundred sheep crossing from one side of Dulun to the other. They ambled along in a lackadaisical manner under the loose direction of a middle-aged Han and his son. I have no idea why they were crossing the street; to me, both sides of the road were indistinguishable. Everything in Dulun—the buildings, the ground, the few clumps of grass—was light brown and frozen.

"The Mongolian and the Tibetan sheep differ in shape and size of tail and in coarseness of wool, the latter having the smaller tail and the longer, coarser wool." I stared at the sheep, concentrating on their tails and the texture of their wool. "The Kazakh sheep is a fat-rumped breed." My problem was a proper frame of reference. To my untrained eye, all of these tails looked small, the wool long and coarse, and each of the rumps wiggling across the broad, dirt road was decidedly fat.

The sheep crossed through the center of Dulun. A double row of poplar trees paralleled the road. Their trunks were painted white and glowed strangely in the sunlit dust that floated everywhere. Lou Shan had stopped here for lunch; Dulun's one restaurant had a menu mounted outside on a board. This public posting of the menu seemed a curiously pretentious touch, bringing to mind a scene of diners strolling through town examining menus as they picked the restaurant of their choice. But Dulun had no choices.

The handwritten characters of the menu detailed three rows of dishes, twenty-seven in all. Sea Cucumber was the most expensive at twenty-seven kuai. I wondered if they really had sea cucumber but I wasn't about to ask. In Xi'an a similar question had resulted in the presentation of the dish by a delighted chef, his obvious pride shaming me into eating most of the long, translucent slug, which resembled a luminous penis.

Bicycles were stacked in front of the restaurant, and a donkey and camel were tied to a post. The camel was secured with leather reins connected to a wooden plug driven through his nose.

Inside the smoky restaurant four flimsy metal tables wobbled in front of a wooden bench. There were no chairs. A particularly friendly Han couple ran the place. He was in his late twenties, his wife younger, with red, round cheeks and delicate eyes. She moved rapidly around the kitchen area in the rear of the room, working over the two metal oil drums, which had been converted into coal-burning stoves. Her hair repeatedly fell out from under her white kerchief, and she pushed it back with a motion that was surprisingly feminine, a link to a different, nonworker self.

Neither the man nor the woman wore worker ID badges.

Mark asked if they owned their restaurant.

While his wife continued her frantic cooking, the man explained that they rented the restaurant space from another work unit. In an embarrassed way, he told us he could make much more money working like this, two or three times the 135-Yuan salary that local workers made. They saved money and sent some to relatives in Szechuan province.

He asked, shyly, to see our van. Lou Shan nodded and led him outside. In his sunglasses, high-heeled black boots, and down parka, Lou Shan cut an impressive figure in Dulun. Strutting proudly, he maneuvered through the large crowd gathered around the vehicle and demonstrated the workings of the double sliding doors, the horn, the smooth throttle of the engine. There were Hans and Tibetans in the crowd.

Outside, we saw several babies dressed in pink jumpsuits with rabbit ears jutting over their tiny faces. Fran liked these very much. The restaurant owner directed us to the place where they were sold.

Dulun's one store reminded me of a rural hardware store. It had a dusty wooden floor and glass cases attended by sleepy old men. They sold old, dusty canned goods wrapped in brown paper with hand-written labels, thick padded Mao jackets, needles, beer, writing tablets . . . and bunny suits. Fran moved through the store trailed by fifteen or twenty people. She found a bunny suit and held it up for a better look. With its dangling feet and flopping ears, I thought it resembled the skin of some grotesque animal. The man behind the counter gestured to the suit and held his hands close together then pointed at Fran and held them far apart. Her collected fans broke out in subdued laughter.

With a repertoire of ardent gestures, Fran tried to explain that she did not plan to wear the suit, that it was for a young cousin. The laughter accelerated and then shifted to cries of interest when she pulled out FEC to pay for the suit.

There are two kinds of currency in China: Renmibi (RMB) and Foreign Exchange Currency (FEC). Renmibi means "People's Money" (just as the Renmin Hotel is the "People's Hotel"). This is a cleverly ironic name because the people don't want Renmibi, they want Foreign Exchange Currency. FEC is the stuff foreigners receive when they exchange money at any Bank of China office, the only place foreigners can legally change money.

The reason the Chinese want FEC is that the government has created a system of stores—Friendship Stores they're called—that sell all the goods everyone wants but can't buy in normal stores. Many of these items would be the sort easily classified as "luxury": Walkman tape players, French perfume, Gillette razors. But many are simply higher quality variations of articles generally available on the street—warmer Mao jackets, better shoes, wool socks. At friendship stores, goods can only be purchased with FEC.

Party cadres apparently have no problem getting FEC. You see them in the Friendship Stores loaded down with cases of Cokes, color televisions, even VCRs (for which, I heard, there is a thriving black market in tapes). The regular Chinese citizen, however, has no legal means for acquiring FEC—so naturally there is a black market in the crisp paper.

The black marketers are mostly a scruffy lot who congregate outside Friendship Stores and in tourist hotels propositioning foreigners. "Change money? Change money?" is their constant refrain. It's not hard to get 130 RMB for 100 FEC, and skillful negotiators have nudged the premium up to 140 RMB.

Some hotels and stores insist foreigners pay for everything with FEC. This is commonly explained as a government policy, but in fact there is no law requiring foreigners to use FEC. The law—rule would be a better word for a country that has no codified legal system—mandates only that foreigners must exchange all their money for FEC. In other words, using RMB is not illegal but *getting* it is. The stores, restaurants, and hotels that insist on FEC often claim it is a regulation, but the people who work there, understandably, are as eager to acquire the precious paper as everyone else.

RMB is about the size of Monopoly money only not quite as substantial in thickness and weight. The thin, crinkly paper is decorated with handsome scenes of an ideological bent: a smiling young girl driving a tractor, a group of happy workers (led by women—China's currency has a distinctively feminist slant) heading into the fields. The smallest denomination of bills features drawings of objects—an airplane, a boat, a truck—caught in a dramatic pose. These bills are called Fens. Ten Fens make up one Jiao and ten Jiao make up one Yuan, commonly called "maos."

FEC, like the goods it will buy, is made from better quality paper with superior printing. It is decorated with landscapes and pagodas, pretty, traditional scenes that would have been destroyed in the Cultural Revolution as links to the feudal past. Now the former Red Guards, many of them cadres, use them to buy VCRs to watch *Rambo,* one of the hot underground tapes on the Beijing scene, favored for its variety and the volume of Vietnamese deaths. The Chinese are still quite sensitive about the drubbing they took during their two-week invasion of Vietnam in 1979.

There are no Friendship Stores in Dulun; the closest was probably in Ürümqi, over a thousand miles away. But Fran's FEC still caused a stir, an ephemeral glimpse into a forbidden, more prosperous world.

At the restaurant we ate a salty omelet and mutton grilled on skewers. Before leaving, we asked the proprietor and his wife to pose for a Polaroid by the van he had admired so much. Both blushed and giggled then assumed rigid poses staring into the distance. When we gave the photo to him, the thirty or forty onlookers pushed in to watch the Polaroid develop. The proprietor, who obviously had experience in these matters, held the photo carefully by the edges and waved it gently to aid drying, pushing the throng away with his other arm. When the picture was completely developed, he handed it to his still blushing wife and darted into his restaurant, coming out with two cans of peaches. He forced these on us despite our protest.

The inevitable industrial commune sat on the edge of town—a five-foot wall surrounding a collection of low, concrete barracks, a pair of smokestacks, and a single massive pile of coal peeking over the walls. SUPPORT THE FOUR MODERNIZATIONS read the slogan over the metal gate.

I asked Lou Shan if he knew what the Four Modernizations were. I actually knew—they were included in every piece of propaganda Beijing produced for foreign consumption, stressing always how much they meant to the common man of China. Lou Shan smiled and looked at me nervously in the rearview mirror.

"I know they are very important," he said, still smiling, His tone was just short of clear mockery. He was testing our reaction. When we laughed, he joined us, looking relieved.

"I can't name the Four Modernizations!" He pronounced proudly. "There is always something the government tells us we should know. Once it was what Chairman Mao said," he shook his head. "Now it's the Four Modernizations. What does this have to do with my life?" He leaned on his horn as the van swerved around a donkey cart with a two-story stack of hay. "Science is one, I think. And agriculture? Does this make me a better driver? Does this make more money for my family?"

We were traveling through a strange and contradictory terrain—the Qaidam Basin. It looked like a desert, flat and monotonous, with scrub grass struggling in the cracked dried earth, and yet stretches of it were covered in light snow. It was a desert but a desert rolled out at nine thousand feet, three thousand feet higher than St. Moritz or Denver. We were in the highest desert in the world.

The Qaidam Basin is a huge divot in the northern slope of the Himalayan mountain plateau. To the south the peaks reached upward like some cheap stage drop, brilliant in the sun, gaudy in their height. These mountains formed the heart of Tibet. Mount Everest is perched a thousand miles away on their southern edge, straddling Tibet and Nepal. Every great river of Asia—the Yellow, the Yangtze, the Indus—begins in these mountains, fed by the glaciers and year-round snowfall.

The Qilian Shan mountain range rose distantly in the north, separating the basin from the more widely traveled Gansu Corridor. In this gulf between two vast ranges, the Qaidam Basin exists as a climatological freak:

The primary factor that effects changes in the weather and climate of this region is the move-

125

> ment of the cold air the year round. . . . The
> cold air from the north often moves in a very
> strong air current that . . . enters the Qaidam
> Basin, bringing a violent fall in temperature,
> gales and dusty weather.

This account from *An Outline of China's Physical Geography* only hints at the strangeness of sand and snow, dry mud flats and salt marshes that are the reality of travel across the basin. It jars all assumptions of the rules of terrain and nature.

We were in a place that had successfully defied the Chinese government's best efforts at forced habitation.

> The government established corps on the
> Qinghai-Tibet Plateau in 1965, to assimilate
> ex-servicemen and settlers (including educated
> young people) from the interior. The chief tar-
> get area of this corps was the Qaidam Basin.
> . . . The cold desert basin of inland drainage in
> the west, in particular, was found to be totally
> uncultivable.

A Dr. Chen Cheng-siang wrote the above in his *Essays on Geography;* he wrote it in English, and the choice of "assimilate" to describe the forced relocation of workers and students is his own.

Occasionally in the distance we saw the low walls of an abandoned agricultural compound swimming in a sea of mirages. A string of camels, a mongol on horseback, two or three yurts, these were the only signs of life across most of the basin.

We stopped in mid-afternoon in an unnamed town for gas. Lou Shan pulled up to a row of red antique pumps in front of a concrete blockhouse. No one was there. We

126

waited while Lou Shan banged on the door. He shrugged apologetically and sat down in the front seat of the van, door open, to have a smoke.

We waited for a long time. The scene had a certain irrepressibly cinematic quality to it: five people gathered around an abandoned gas station in the Chinese desert, endless vistas of parched scrub grass on all sides, towering mountains playing in the background. David did push-ups. Fran listened to the Talking Heads, Mark stared off in space, probably thinking about his girlfriend, and Lou Shan smoked. I walked in circles around the gas station.

At some point—I had steeled myself against looking at my watch—Lou Shan closed the van door and drove off. Cinematic mood intact, we watched it disappear down the bombed-out main street of the dusty town in silence.

I wandered off behind the gas station where a maze of crumbling mud walls surrounded the ruins of what might have once been a warehouse. I wondered if the faded Chinese characters painted on the walls were remnants of the Red Guard's appearance fifteen years ago. It was difficult to imagine a place more in keeping with the Great Proletarian Cultural Revolution than this forgotten petrol oasis.

One mud wall was pocked with patterns of tiny holes at irregular intervals. They looked exactly like shotgun blasts.

I walked hurriedly back to the front of the gas station. Lou Shan had returned with two young PLA soldiers. They looked embarrassed and when one passed near me to unlock the hose of the pump, I smelled liquor on his breath. Lou Shan scolded them, grinning in his sly hipster manner.

Tanks full, we left the soldiers standing by the pumps.

* * *

Golmud rises out of the desert in the same sudden, surprising way as Las Vegas. All comparisons end there.

It was a little after 6:00 P.M. when Lou Shan stopped at a hotel next to a railroad siding. It was a large three-story concrete building with unexpectedly fashionable floor to ceiling glass panels, all broken, in the lobby. Uneven concrete split by wide cracks covered the floor. Behind the desk two women seemed shocked to see us.

All day we had talked about getting to Golmud in time to go to the CITS office. Though we were still in Qinghai province, it was not far to the Xinjiang border and we hoped the office might be able to make arrangements for us to continue westward along Fleming and Maillart's route. In Xinning, Kahn had suggested that this might be possible, indicating that the Golmud CITS office was known to be particularly helpful. It seemed logical that out here on the rough edges of civilization, rules and Public Security officials would have less sway.

Mark asked the girls behind the desk what time the CITS office closed. They looked even more shocked and barked answers in unison, casting suspicious glances at us.

"They say there isn't a CITS office here."

We were silent. Another burst of Chinese came from behind the desk.

"And they say we can't stay in this hotel because we're foreigners."

"Is there another hotel for foreigners?" I asked. "Maybe a Sheraton?"

"With a pool," Fran added.

Mark asked, then listened to a very long monologue from one of the girls.

"No." He said in a very tired voice. "They say this is the only hotel in Golmud."

Lou Shan returned from the bathroom in the hall and immediately started in with the girls in a loud voice.

"He's asking the girls where we should go if they refuse to take us. Don't they understand that we are important guests and part of the Four Modernizations is welcoming foreign guests?"

I was getting to like Lou Shan.

David and I wandered outside where it was distinctly warmer. The hotel had no heat and functioned like a giant refrigerator. Two ragged Muslim children walked behind their mother who carried a load of coal on her head. The desert began a few hundred yards away.

Inside, the argument had been joined by a middle-aged man with the look of a cadre. He wore a clean Mao jacket and black plastic gloves made in a imitation lizard skin pattern.

David suggested to Mark that we stay some place closer to the train station so that we could find out about trains out of Golmud more easily. We were all aware that Lou Shan would be leaving the next morning to return to Xinning without us.

Fran and I seconded this idea. "But we just had this big argument with the clerks," Mark answered, "because there isn't any other place in Golmud to stay. This is it."

"Mark, we've got to try and stay closer to the center of town," I said. "We've got to find out about buses and trains. Somewhere there's a truck depot, and we need to go there and talk to drivers. We can't do that from here."

The thought of all those questions to be posed caused Mark's already unhappy visage to sink even lower. He took off his huge furry gloves and pushed his PLA hat with the flying flaps back off his head.

Sighing, he started back into the conversation, which

129

still raged. His comments silenced the desk girls, the cadre, and Lou Shan.

When he finished, Mark shuffled off toward the van. "I told them we wouldn't stay here," he said over his shoulder. "Lou Shan will take us to the bus station. Maybe we'll just sleep in the van, I don't know."

We drove farther into Golmud. The town was laid out in a grid of dirt streets lined with half-finished concrete apartment buildings and mud houses. At the main intersection, two camels were tied to a statue of a Han couple carrying hoes. For the first time in China, I saw army troops carrying rifles on patrol.

The bus station was set off from the main street along a circular driveway. Two surprisingly modern buses were parked outside the door; a group of Tibetans stood looking at the buses. We pushed through the open doorway covered by two blankets strung together.

The building seemed to be marginally heated though it may have been just the result of so many bodies pressed together. We were in a foyer with two long corridors lined with doors branching off of either end. A man sat in a room with a glass window. There was a tiny hole cut into the glass.

Mark leaned down and spoke loudly through the window. The man waved and smiled. Mark spoke louder.

"What is this place?" David asked.

"He doesn't know anything about buses," Mark reported. He was sweating under the rabbit fur of his PLA hat. The Tibetans had latched onto Fran, crowding around.

Anarchy was very near.

"Buses leave for Lasha every two days at 5:30 in morning. Tickets advance." David read from a handwritten card stuck under the glass of the front counter.

"It's in English?" I asked stupidly.

"You know what this is?" Fran said. "This is a hotel." She had wandered down one of the long halls to escape the staring Tibetans.

Mark shouted a question through the glass window. "It's a hotel," he confirmed.

We filled out registration cards, each receiving a little red plastic folder with our room number. They looked like the ID cards all Chinese were required to carry. Three young female attendants eventually appeared, clustered around a tall man in his mid-twenties who wore a blue-jean jacket and high leather boots. He looked part Muslim and part Han, with long black hair swept off to the side of his head. He spoke a little English.

"Where you from?" he asked, cocking his head and putting his hands on his hips. He shook hands with Lou Shan. The two seemed to like each other immediately. Standing together, the two hipsters looked like a Chinese rock duo.

He introduced himself as Bai Shiuhua. He took the keys from one of the attendants and led us down the hall.

The hall bathrooms were doorless; two Tibetan men and a PLA soldier squatted over slits in the floor as we walked past. Water ran out of the bathroom into the hall. It was all beginning to seem terribly familiar.

The rooms were six yuan without rug and nine with rug. We splurged. Our hipster friend led us into the rooms. I asked him about buses. He frowned.

"Bus here."

"These are buses to Lasha. We want to go west, are there other buses?"

He cocked his head quizzically, and Mark stepped in to help.

An excited exchange followed. We moved into one

of the small rooms and showed Bai Shiuhua, on our map, the thin red road we wanted to follow west to the edge of the Takla Makan. He nodded vigorously.

"This is great," Mark said. "He says there is definitely a bus that goes that way."

"Can foreigners take it?" Fran asked.

"He says no one cares what you do. But really I don't think he would know about that. He's not an official or anything."

In the hallway, we shook hands and thanked him. He was very nonchalant.

After a bleak dinner of stringy chicken and sandy rice, Mark, David, and I headed off to find the bus station. Fran, in no mood to be followed by an admiring throng, stayed at the hotel.

Bai Shiuhua had given very precise instructions on how to find the bus station. They seemed quite simple. Forty minutes later we had retraced them twice from the hotel without success. It was dark, and there were no street signs. We found ourselves debating the differences between an alley and a street.

"He said three streets to the left."

"Street? You think this is a street?"

Finally we returned to the hotel, where Lou Shan was chatting with an attractive female desk clerk. Mark explained what we were trying to do. After a talk with the girl, Lou Shan told us that the bus station was on the opposite side of town. Once there had been another station where we had looked but now it was closed. At least she thought a station had been there. But in any event, she explained, Bai Shiuhua didn't know where the bus station was. He had never been in Golmud before.

But we thought he worked here?

The girl giggled, covering her mouth with her hand.

He was a tourist, she said. He had been staying at the hotel for some time.

A tourist in Golmud?

She nodded.

Why had Bai Shiuhua given us directions if he didn't know what he was talking about?

She giggled again. He was from Beijing, she explained.

Someone came all the way from Beijing to stay here? Why?

But you, Lou Shan pointed out, had come all the way from America.

We thought about this while listening to new directions from the girl.

Outside the hotel, the Tibetans still stood and stared at the two empty buses. It was dark now and fiercely cold.

Lou Shan had told us the new station was only four streets away. It turned out this was true but the streets were almost a half mile apart. We walked the route in silence, coughing in the dust. It seemed like a long time ago that we had been excited hearing about the station and the buses heading west.

Down a wide side street, we found a dozen old buses parked at random. The street was lined with one-story brick buildings that all looked alike. It was very dark and if there was a sign identifying one of the buildings as the bus station, we couldn't find it.

An alley between two of the buildings opened into a mud parking lot filled with trucks. Behind a side door facing onto the parking lot we could hear laughter and music. Standing by their machines smoking, a group of truck drivers eyed us suspiciously, their cigarettes glowing in the darkness.

"I'll just go ask," Mark said lightly, walking toward

the side door that was lit by a single bulb dangling from a bare electrical pole. It was a decidedly gutsy move. David and I murmured encouragement.

The door opened to what seemed to be a Chinese fraternity party. Mark was swept inside. David and I looked at each other, both feeling a little queasy.

"He'll be fine," David said without much conviction.

"Of course," I agreed.

We waited, half expecting to see the door fly open and a rowdy group of Chinese giving Mark the heave-ho. The truck parking lot was enclosed on two sides by long, low-slung buildings that resembled an abandoned motel in the Tennessee hills. There were twenty or so trucks parked in the open space.

This was a lucky break. Without looking for it, we apparently had stumbled across the truck depot we had wanted to find. Map in hand, David and I approached a group of drivers.

We offered Marlboro cigarettes. None were accepted but they brought tentative smiles. With body English and a few shared words of Chinese and English, we established that they were indeed drivers and we might be able to ride with them. We were just rolling out the map to examine it under the headlights of a truck, when Mark came out of the side door. He was laughing and looked a little drunk.

"Any luck?" David asked hopefully.

"None. Absolutely none. They sure are nice guys, though."

Shaking hands all around, Mark introduced himself to our companions.

"Who are these guys?" he asked us between bursts of Chinese.

"We think they're truck drivers. We were just trying to figure out if they were headed west."

At their insistence, we moved inside one of the rooms framing the parking lot. About a dozen men crowded into the small square room. The smoke from the coal stove in the center made it look like an old lithograph of an opium den. The apparent leader sat behind a flimsy desk. He had long hair and high cheekbones, a handsome man with a passing resemblance to Gregory Peck. His position behind the desk gave the proceedings a strangely formal air.

We squeezed out a place on one of the straw cots. We offered Marlboros. They were refused. Mark began to charm the crowd. He did so very quickly. Within a few moments he had everyone laughing; a bottle of baijo made the rounds. The map came out, and our route was explained.

These were rough, big-handed men, with none of the palpable sloth of the cadres and CITS officials we had come to know. They took obvious pride in their knowledge of the road and its hazards.

Yes, they all had trucks and yes, it might be possible for us to ride with one of them. But none of them were going west. Only someone going to Kashgar would be heading in that direction, and no trucks from this area went to Kashgar. You would have to go north to Ürümqi to find a truck headed to Kashgar.

Would it be possible for us to hire one of their trucks to drive us even if it was out of the way?

After much consultation, it was the general consensus that the one road west out of Golmud became impassable long before it connected with the southern route around the Takla Makan. No one used it regularly, they explained, so it was not maintained. Did we understand that this was in the great desert and very hard to travel?

We understood.

They suggested we try the bus ticket window across

the street, a different office than the one Mark had entered. We shook hands and left.

"You know what I like about those guys," Mark said as we walked across the street. "All the time we were talking, nobody ever used the word 'forbidden.' Nobody said we were forbidden to go on the southern route or it wasn't allowed because we were foreigners. With them it was just a question of practicality. They couldn't take us because they weren't going that way and the roads are bad. It was almost like a normal conversation. How amazing."

Behind the tiny ticket window, a red light burned. Someone was asleep on a cot next to a stove. We tapped on the glass with no effect. We walked through an open doorway next to the window leading into a large office where schedules were posted. In an adjoining room, a group of men watched "I Dream of Jeannie" on television. They gawked as we appeared, perhaps thinking we were more mischief conjured up by Barbara Eden.

When Mark began to speak Chinese with the fluency of Larry Hagman's dubbed voice, the crowd rushed forward. The map came out, and the usual questions began.

After fifteen minutes, the bus work unit cadre, a schedule brigade leader, a driver, two drunks, and a chain-smoking PLA transport captain each had different opinions of our plight. Whenever Kashgar was mentioned, a stunned pause would follow and then a deafening cacophony of sharp voices. In the end, all agreed on one point—we couldn't get there from here. Kashgar might as well been the far side of the moon.

Chapter Sixteen

"We've got to talk," Mark said as we were walking back to our awful hotel. "All along I've said that I won't do anything illegal in China. I said that back in America."

I agreed.

"Look, we've found out there are no buses heading west. We talked to the truck drivers, and we can't go with them. We've done everything that you wanted to do, everything we *could* do. I've tried to help."

In his willingness to throw himself into the fray all evening, Mark had gone above and beyond the call. David and I expressed our appreciation. I knew how much he hated having to press people for details and answers and he had done more than a fair bit of pressing.

"What I'm worried about is that you're going to do something crazy now," Mark blurted. "I know how much you want to stay on Fleming's route but this is it, we're stuck."

"You don't think we could spend some time here and try to find somebody we could pay to take us in a car?"

"Spend time in Golmud? You are crazy. And who has a car?"

"We can't stay here," David asserted. "I don't care where we go, but not here. This is the worst place I've ever been in my life."

David gestured around us. We stood in front of a

rubble of concrete that might have been a building going up or it might have been a building coming down. Much of Golmud was in this ambiguous transition stage.

"We've got to get to some town with a CITS office where we might be able to get a car," David said.

"The closest place is Dunhuang," Mark suggested. "I'm pretty sure there would be a CITS office there. People go there to see the Buddhist caves. And I think we can take a bus there. It was on the schedule in that office."

Dunhuang was due north toward Ürümqi. "How long does the bus take?" I asked.

"Two or three days, I think," Mark said.

No one said anything for a moment.

"It doesn't matter how long it takes," David said. "We don't have any choice. We either take that bus or we go back, that's it."

Back at the Nightmare Inn, we spread our Bartholomew map out on the bed. If we could get to Dunhuang, we might be able to take a road that branched southwest from the town to the Takla Makan. Our destination, as far as I was concerned, was still the southern half of the road that circled the desert. That would take us through Hotan, Qiemo, Yecheng, the same string of oasis towns Fleming and Maillart traveled through to Kashgar.

"But the truck drivers said that road was closed," Mark said.

"I thought it was just the portion of the road from Golmud to here." I pointed to the road from Golmud west to the desert.

Lou Shan slid in wearing sunglasses. Had he said, "What's happening, baby?" I would have been only marginally surprised.

"Mark, ask Lou Shan if we could pay him a small fortune to drive us to Kashgar."

Mark glared at me but posed the question.

Lou Shan snorted in an amused way.

"He says he would love to do so but he would have no life if he did."

"That's probably the truth," David said solemnly.

We agreed that first thing in the morning we would try and find out more about buses to Dunhuang.

The next morning at breakfast, I ran into an American and Canadian who had arrived at the Xinning Binguan our last day. The American's name was Lee Richards. He had wavy blond hair slicked back in a modified pompadour and wore gold chains and a thick gold ID bracelet with his initials. He was somewhere in his late thirties and seemed a most unlikely sort of fellow to be wandering around the back wastes of China.

His traveling companion was more in keeping with the stock youth-hostel image—mid-twenties, bearded, wearing a parka with a Greenpeace insignia on the sleeve.

"We were on the train all night," Lee said. "It was so goddamn cold, I think my balls turned to ice cubes."

"What happened to you?" the Canadian, Marty, asked.

"Me?"

"You look worse than we do. And I know you weren't on the train. This town must be getting to you."

"Beat just like a borrowed mule, is what you look," Lee laughed. He was from Marietta, Georgia, near Atlanta and was not the first Atlanta businessman I'd met who liked to play the country boy. Lee was a former computer salesman.

"Must be this hotel," Marty said. "You catch the smell in the halls?"

"Doesn't matter to me," Lee insisted. "We're out of here at 5:30 tomorrow morning. Next stop, Lhasa."

"Actually, they stop for the night someplace," Marty corrected him. "Someplace in the middle of nowhere, I hear. Now that's when you better mind your balls don't turn to ice."

"Look at those goddamn Hans," Lee nodded toward a table of laughing PLA soldiers. He leaned down and whispered, "You hear anything about some Australians smuggling rifles to Tibet?"

Instantly I thought of Nicki, the punk rocker, the only Australian I'd met in China. "Guns to Tibet?" I asked.

Lee nodded conspiratorially. "Brought 'em in for gold, we heard. Tibetans still got gold stashed, you know. Hans didn't get everything. Word is the Han border troops and Public Security are bustin' their ass looking for 'em."

"Some Marine told us this in Xinning," Marty explained. "Seemed like a bit of a Rambo to me."

"A bit?" Lee hooted. "Fuckin' A. a bit. This guy was Rambo right from the get-go. You know what the silly muther's wearing around China?"

I didn't.

"An 82nd Airborne T-shirt with KILL 'EM ALL AND LET GOD SORT IT OUT big as Jesus right on the front. Too bad it's not in characters so the Han brethren could appreciate it."

"Actually," Marty said, just as our fried bread arrived. "That's really a very Buddhist concept."

"I hear Tibet is a very spiritual place," Lee nodded with conviction. "You can just look at those Tibetans and tell they are operating on a level we can't even begin to understand."

"I have never seen a people look more helpless in all my life," Marty said.

"The Hans eat 'em for breakfast."

I paused with a bread stick halfway to my mouth.

Lee continued. "They don't even think the Tibetans are human. You know what racists they are."

"Tell him about the student in Beijing," Marty urged.

"We met this student in Beijing. Seemed like a nice guy, not one of these "Change Money" kind of creeps. We get to talking and when I tell him I'm from the South, he asks me," Lee slipped into a sing-song voice, "why do Americans treat blacks like slaves?"

Marty started laughing.

"Look, it's not the first time I've had to defend the South, right? So I start in with all the usual lines and then he says—I swear to God—'You know blacks, they are gorillas.' "

Marty howled.

"So I figure maybe he's trying to be cute or something, so I sort of laugh and then this fucker, he gets real serious like and tells me, 'It is true. It is why Chinese are so much smarter than anyone else. We are the least like apes. Blacks are still apes!' "

"But not slaves," Marty said.

"Fuckin' A. Apes" Lee yelled across the room at the PLA soldiers, "No apes in Golmud, huh boys? Killed 'em all for Mao, right?" He shook his head and squeezed off a bit of the fried bread. "There anything to do in this dump for fun?"

By noon we had the scoop on buses: a two-day trip from Golmud to Dunhuang. It cost 18 yuan—a little over $5.00.

"That's some kind of bargain," I noted.

"You didn't see the buses," Fran said.

"The ones in front of the hotel are kind of nice."

"Yes, they are. The ones at the bus station aren't."

"I think the buses we saw might just be the ones they use for short trips," Mark suggested. "The long-haul buses are probably better."

There was one other bit of news about the bus situation.

"We have to stay here three days," David reported glumly.

"Three days?"

It was true. The run to Dunhuang was a twice weekly event, and we had just missed a bus.

"Three days in Golmud," David said flatly.

"If we're going to spend three days here," Fran said, "we've got to make some friends."

"Friends?"

"I'm serious. We need to meet some people. If we just hang around this hotel for three days, we'll drive each other crazy."

So we met some people. Or Mark and David did, rather, and introduced Fran and me.

Li Xain Hua was the headmaster of Golmud's only school. He was a Han, thirty-six, a bookish man of considerable charm and intensity. A man hard not to like.

Mark and David stumbled across the school while out surveying the town. On a whim they stopped, fell into conversation with some teachers, and soon had met Li Xain Hua. Hearing about Mark's teaching days at Hunan Medical College, Li Xain Hua invited us all back to talk to one of their English classes.

The school looked like every small industrial commune we'd seen in China. There was a low concrete wall surrounding a collection of one-story buildings in a courtyard of packed dirt. A camel was tied to the metal gate, which was adorned with the standard red stars and a slogan: FERVENTLY SEEK PROGRESS.

We jammed into Li Xain Hua's small office tacked onto one of the classrooms. It had an uneven brick floor and broken windows covered with paper; a charcoal stove stuffed to capacity kept it uncomfortably warm, a sensation I'd almost forgotten.

Li Xain Hua had come to Golmud four years earlier—by choice, he was careful to point out. In Golmud, he made more money, he said matter of factly—220 yuan a month instead of the 135 he was making in Hunan province.

But it was when talking about what he could accomplish in Golmud that Li Xain Hua became excited.

"Before the Cultural Revolution, all we studied was Russian and Russian ways. We had a Five Year Plan for everything. Then in the Cultural Revolution we didn't study anything. For ten years this died—" He tapped his head, grinning slyly. "Now we study English."

"I've heard," Fran said, "that there are more people studying English in China than in America."

Li Xain Hua and his teachers laughed in an embarrassed but pleased way. "This is probably true. You see, China has a great past but the light of our future will outshine even the brightest days of the glorious past. And education is the key." He struck his fist in his palm, staring at us intently.

"Here in the West, this is where China's new greatness lies. We have oil, minerals, vast lands."

You could read what Li Xain Hua was saying in any issue of *Beijing Review;* it was the official line. But this intelligent, quick man actually believed it, making the words come alive. It was as startling as meeting someone in the New York subway declaiming on the excellence of the city's mass transit planning.

Later, Mark taught a class of some forty teen-aged students. He was dazzling, quickly leading the shy, hesitant class into a rollicking discussion of Chinese-American customs. Afterward, the students pressed around him for autographs, some reaching out just to touch him, like a rock star.

It was the first time Mark had looked truly happy since we arrived in China.

When we left, a detail of students spread out over the school yard, sprinkling water from rusty cans onto the dirt, trying, with little effect, to reduce the thick dust that floated everywhere.

Chapter
Seventeen

We walked to the bus in cold darkness, shuffling quietly through the empty dirt streets. It was 5:30 A.M.

With our heavy bags, it took forty minutes to reach the station. We heard the bus before we saw it or rather heard the angry squabbling of passengers. In the total darkness of the street, the bus was invisible until we were right beside it.

Under the flicker of our flashlights, it looked as if the bus was under attack. Several PLA soldiers knelt on top of the machine, casually pushing aside boxes and bags in the luggage rack to make room for their own, while frantic civilians tried to scale the roof ladder hanging down the rear of the bus. A soldier squatted at the top of the ladder rhythmically flailing the attempted boarders with a rolled-up magazine.

Another minor riot was underway at the bus door where five or six people tried to squeeze inside at once. Each person carried either a burlap bag or a large cardboard box, some both, making entrance all the more unlikely.

With foolish optimism, I looked around in hope of spotting another bus. I had a vision of a mighty Trailways, clean and new, with wide seats, a floor not drenched in spit, and maybe even a bathroom. And heat, God, yes, heat, and windows that weren't broken and—

David yelled to me to hand up our bags. He had somehow commandeered a position at the top of the roof-ladder. We passed the bags to him, and I scrambled up to help secure them under a rope net stretched over the metal rack. My bag was jammed next to a wooden crate holding a smallish pig; the creature seemed strangely calm considering his likely future as a pork icicle. The little thermometer I carried read 12 degrees.

Like many encounters of sudden violence, I can't recall how we managed to fit into the bus. The bench seats were narrow and short, a squeeze for two people. Each held three. I ended up wedged next to the window with two PLA soldiers muscling in next to me. David and Mark were one row ahead and Fran was across the aisle hanging onto the end of a seat.

A half dozen people stood in the aisle.

A thick layer of frost covered the window next to my ear. After the bickering over seats and luggage, the bus turned quiet. A faint trace of exhaust fumes floated through the interior, then vanished under the assault of cold air that rushed through the window cracks as the bus began to move.

Within ten minutes I began to wonder if I would last through the hour. With the wind chill the temperature must have been close to zero. The only thing keeping me from hypothermia was the effort expended pushing against the soldier next to me who appeared determined to shove me out the broken window. The battle was a welcome diversion. My opponent seemed surprised that I resisted his eviction; he grunted periodically, assaulting me with his fierce garlic breath.

Almost everyone on the bus wore a surgical mask. Before coming to China, I'd read that these masks were sometimes worn but I was unprepared for their impact. In a country in which social pressure—and poverty—mandated dressing alike, the masks struck me as the final step in an earnest attempt to remove all traces of individuality.

Through the blasts of garlic and the acrid smoke of Chinese cigarettes, I smelled a distinctive, pungent odor. My seat companion stopped elbowing me and together we sniffed. There was something about the smell that was familiar, something non-Chinese.

"Good God," I cried, "my shoe is melting!"

I jumped to my feet, smashing my head.

Cursing, I lunged into the aisle, hurling myself over my seat companions. Laughter rocked the bus. Hopping on one foot, I ripped off my shoe. Fran used her flashlight to illuminate the sole. It looked like it had been branded with a long bar.

I flashed the light down on the floor. A long metal tube stretched along the base of the bus wall. It was bare, bright steel ventilated with holes. Holding my hand directly over it, I could feel its intense heat but the bus's broken windows and holes in the chassis floor and wall sucked the radiant warmth straight outside. As a heating device the contraption was completely useless but as an instrument of torture, it held possibilities.

Still mumbling curses, I pushed the two soldiers over and perched on the edge of the seat. The soldiers immediately fell asleep, leaning their heads together like lovers.

False dawn began to brighten the sky. We were heading due north. The road was perfectly straight but there were rolling arid hills on both sides and high mountains straight ahead. Golmud was located on the southern edge of the Quadim Basim and the road to Dunhuang went across the basin and over the Qilian Shan Mountains.

If it was this cold in the desert, I wondered how it would be bearable in the mountains. Mark, David, Fran, and I were all equipped with expensive American high-tech gear but some people on the bus wore only padded cotton Mao jackets.

Across the narrow aisle, Fran had removed her boots and stuck her feet in a pair of heavy down gloves.

Tired of bouncing off my few inches of seat at every bump, I moved down into the doorway and sat on the steps. The double doors in front of me swung open constantly, assaulting me with clouds of dust and frigid air. I turned sideways, pulled my hat down low and fell asleep.

I woke up in a nightmare of screams and laughter. A woman directly over me was jumping up and down and yelling; everyone thought this was very funny.

"What's going on?" I shouted to Mark.

"She has to go to the bathroom. She says if the driver doesn't stop she's going to do it right here."

My head was inches from the woman's knees. I struggled up just as the bus hit a bump. Behind me the doors flapped open, and I lurched backward into space. Fran reached out and grabbed my arm.

The woman who needed to go to the bathroom stopped yelling and started laughing.

The driver, an amiable middle-aged Han with a jaunty English-style driving cap, ground the bus to a halt.

I fell off the bus backward into a scene so primeval I had to smile.

A great red ball of a sun rose over a flat brown landscape of dirt and scrub. It looked just like the backdrop in the dinosaur exhibit at the Natural History Museum. Except for the bus and the road—and both barely qualified—there was nothing to suggest man's presence for hundreds of miles.

As if by prearrangement, the men used one side of

the road as a toilet, the women the other. There was nothing to hide behind, and no one seemed to mind.

David knocked off a couple of hundred pushups in the dirt. By the time he finished, he had intimidated most of the bus. For the rest of the trip, people shyed away from him, like New Yorkers on a subway wary of a potentially violent and deranged rider.

The last to reboard, I nestled down on the steps and tried to concentrate on Ross Macdonald's *Zebra-Striped Hearse.* There was something very pleasing in reading about California's decadent prosperity, drugs, and sex. The book was like an encyclopedia of Chinese criticisms of Western life. I found this comforting.

We stopped in a small town of mud houses for lunch. Two pigs were engaged in a lengthy race down the single street. Three pretty girls—a startling sight—strolled hand in hand. As if on command, they each spit into the dirt. The town's only restaurant served steaming plates of jiaozi, dumplings stuffed with pork. Actually procuring the food was a typically complicated maneuver. It required the purchase of a ticket at one line, the presentation of the ticket at another, and the awarding of food at yet a third. In the narrow restaurant, the three lines were desperately confused. Everyone yelled a lot.

The other diners were skilled in a repertoire of tricks to advance their position in line. Though we had been among the first to queue up, most everyone had been served while we were still lost somewhere between the second and third lines. The female conductor from the bus intervened, barking and pushing until we had our full bowls of steamy dough.

Bus conductors in China are a special breed. All are female, and all whom I encountered were tough and competent. Inexplicably, most seem to be pretty and young.

Perhaps it was seen as a glamorous job, the airline stewardess of the Third World.

The conductor on the Golmud to Dunhuang run wore high-heeled boots and a white sweatshirt with two tennis rackets embroidered at a suggestive angle. She spoke a few words of English, and we tried to talk while standing outside the restaurant, both clicking away with chopsticks at our plates of dumplings. The bus had stopped for over an hour, and I was worried about the delay. I had a desperate interest in doing everything I could to speed the trip.

Pointing to my watch and saying "Dunhuang?" in a questioning manner, I queried her about when we might arrive.

Eight o'clock, she pointed to the numbers on my watch face.

With a looping motion, I confirmed she meant eight o'clock tomorrow, not today.

This was confusing. She finally seemed to comprehend and shook her head vigorously. Eight o'clock tonight, she seemed to be saying.

Afraid to believe this incredibly good news, I rushed to grab Mark. "I think this woman is trying to tell me we get to Dunhuang today, not tomorrow."

Mark scrambled out to confirm. It was true.

Climbing back on the bus, I felt like a death row convict who had just gotten a call from the governor's office.

"What's wrong with your pants," Fran asked. She was behind me in line to get on the bus.

"What do you mean?"

"Look," she said, brushing the seat of my corduroys. "They're wet."

"Wet?" I reached around and felt a sticky, embarrassing dampness.

"You know what I think it is?" She said this in the horrified but amused tone people use when they talk about grotesque car wrecks.

I didn't, and I was pretty sure I didn't want to either.

She pointed down to the floor of the bus where I'd been sitting. It was covered in spit. I could feel a sticky coldness beginning to soak through my long underwear.

That afternoon we climbed out of the flat basin over the western edge of the Qilian Shan Mountains. The bus shuddered over the high pass, slipping precariously backward as the driver fought the gears. The mountains were unlike any I'd ever seen. Over fifteen thousand feet, they were higher than the Colorado Rockies and yet they remained as arid and bleak as the desert. The temperature in the bus dropped to 15 degrees as, gears grinding and engine whining, we crept through the snowless terrain.

All day we passed trucks broken down in the middle of the road. As soon as a vehicle was visible—frequently miles ahead—the driver leaned on his horn. This continued until we had passed the truck in question. Since the vehicles were disabled and couldn't move, it was impossible for them to respond to our extended warning. The real purpose of the horn blowing, I decided, was to alert everyone on the bus that something worth seeing was up ahead while lending a certain gaiety to the occasion. The Chinese have a highly developed appreciation for vehicular misfortune, the more grisly the better. Our fellow passengers would grow quite animated, delighted with the break in the afternoon's monotony.

Not long after lunch, we stopped to pick up a peasant standing by the road. We were miles from any semblance of civilization, but no one appeared surprised to come upon this old man wearing rags and carrying a huge burlap bag and two buckets balanced on a pole, coolie-style, on his shoulders. He struggled through the door and collapsed in my former position in the stairwell (I had moved to a seat to avoid the liquid hazards.)

Hours later, the peasant took off his tattered PLA hat to reveal a pigtail. I pondered for a long time whether this meant that he was a woman, or just an old-fashioned male peasant. But when the doors swung open, as was their want, and the peasant screeched at the driver in a high voice, I decided it was a female.

Hovering in the doorway, holding on to a seat brace with one hand, the woman pulled a bent spoon out of her ripped Mao jacket and began to eat something out of one of the buckets. It was a grayish-white gel, and it took me a while to realize she was eating lard. She had no teeth but worked her gums actively to ingest the fat.

Later, on the outskirts of Dunhuang, she began to shriek at the driver. Apparently she wanted him to stop before driving into the center of town. Everyone laughed as her pleas escalated to screams. She shook the railing by the steps and rocked back and forth like an angry child.

The driver did finally stop but only briefly and when he pulled away, she was halfway out the door, pulling hard on her massive burlap sack, the buckets carried on her shoulder banging wildly against her face. She tumbled backward onto the road as the bus pulled away, her sack landing on top of her.

The bus moved into Dunhuang.

Chapter
Eighteen

Peter Fleming never came to Dunhuang but by 1935, many Westerners had. They came—the Chinese insist—to loot.

It was the Caves of 1,000 Buddhas that brought, successively, the Budapest-born, English scholar Sir Aurel Stein, the Frenchman Paul Pelliot, and Harvard professor Langdon Warner to this oasis surrounded by massive sand dunes.

> Here, carved in irregular rows into the cliff are more than four hundred ancient rock temples and chapels. The greatest and most extensive—it stretches for a mile—of all Central Asia's *ming-oi,* or rock temple complexes, it was for centuries renowned throughout the Buddhist world as a centre for prayer and thanksgiving. . . . Enshrined there today are the paintings and sculptures of more than fifteen hundred years. "A great art gallery in the desert" is Mildred Cable's description.

This was from a book called *Foreign Devils on the Silk Road,* which I read our first night in Dunhuang. The author, Peter Hopkirk, explained that the name Dunhuang means "blazing beacon." This was appropriate as the oasis was either the first or the last stop—depending on one's direction—for caravans crossing the Takla Makan desert. "Because it was the point where the northern and southern arms of the Silk Road converged," Hopkirk wrote, "all travellers coming to or from China by the overland route had to pass through Dunhuang. As a result of this heavy caravan and pilgrim traffic, the oasis itself acquired considerable prosperity over the centuries. . . ."

Reading about Dunhuang—that pleasant oasis of "considerable prosperity"—and walking through it induced a schizophrenic confusion that I was coming to expect in China. Almost everything you read about China and the actual physical reality of the post-Cultural Revolution world are wildly different. I frequently had this sense that I was trying to find my way through 1945 Berlin with a 1938 guide. For understandable reasons, most books on China celebrate its past without mentioning very much about the present. I was learning that there seemed to be a direct correlation between the degree a city's past was touted and the awfulness of its present condition. (Golmud is an exception—it had no past to celebrate and still has an awful present.) Fodor's guide, for example, describes at length the Caves of 1,000 Buddhas, but notes about Dunhuang itself only that "it is not easy to reach."

It was true that being "not easy to reach" was the first thing you noticed about Dunhuang. The second had to be the loudspeakers.

Mounted on bare wooden poles all over the town, they blared propaganda songs like "Socialism is joy" interrupted by a squeaky female voice exhorting the Dunhuang throngs to collective greatness: "Comrades! A better China is your responsibility!" Though the volume was deafening, no one seemed to acknowledge the noise in any way.

"Doesn't it bother you?" I asked the young CITS official our first morning in town. "All that noise?"

"What noise?"

"The speakers."

"Americans like music, I think. May I help you settle your itinerary? Dunhuang is an oasis town. An oasis is a peace island in a sea of dry sand. On your itinerary, you will see many high sand mountains. These are named dunes and—"

"Actually," I interrupted, "we wanted to talk to you about making travel arrangements."

"A itinerary. Yes." She smiled, brushing back her wavy hair.

"A long-distance itinerary is what we had in mind." Out came the worn map and my explanation of how we wanted to travel on the Southern Silk Road through Hotan to Kashgar.

"There is bus from Ürümqi to Kashgar," she suggested.

I found myself making up new wrinkles. "Yes, but we've already done that," I lied. "You see, Ürümqi to Kashgar is on the northern route, and while we enjoyed it very much, we do not want to do this twice."

She nodded knowingly. "I must speak with my director."

"Is he here?"

"He has Political Study Meeting."

"How long does that take? We would like to arrange our itinerary as soon as possible."

"Political Study takes all day."

There seemed nothing to do. We moved on to discussing when we might be able to see the caves.

A short man in his late thirties walked in. He was a gentle-looking sort in a blue sweater and gray pants. He was the first person I'd seen in Dunhuang wearing Western clothes.

"This is the director," the young official said calmly.

Mark took the lead as the director spoke no English. I heard the phrase "American desert." The director nodded agreeably.

"He wants to know how much we could pay for a car," Mark told me, smiling. "It looks like we can do it."

"To take a car from here south along the desert?"

"That's what he says. He has four-wheel-drive jeeps, just what we need."

As we began to negotiate the price, three scruffy Hans walked into the office. They belonged to the Car Brigade. Immediately, all began to offer their opinions on the feasibility of our proposal. Everyone in the room, except Mark and I, talked at once.

Finally the Car Brigade leader indicated he would settle the matter once and for all. He picked up the phone. "Wei! Wei!" he shouted.

He held the phone out at arm's length, stared at it, then hung up. In a moment it began to ring. He picked it up and bellowed his way into a conversation. As he talked, the phone continued to ring. Everyone else in the room raised their voices to compete with the phone and the shouting into the receiver. In the low-ceilinged, concrete room, the sound was tremendous.

Eventually, the director announced that they couldn't drive us.

"Why?" I directed my question to the female CITS official.

"It is not possible for our Unit to buy fuel in Xinjiang province," she responded after an exchange with the director.

"Have you ever been allowed to buy gas in that province?"

"No."

"Then why did you think that you might be able to do it? To get to Kashgar from here, you have to drive over 2,000 kilometers in Xinjiang province. Obviously you would need to buy gas along the way."

Had a UFO landed in the office and Chairman Mao walked out shouting, "Wei! Wei!" their looks of astonishment could not have been greater. Puzzled discussion commenced around the room.

"Turpan," I sighed, referring to another oasis town farther north, "is in Xinjiang province, yes?"

She nodded happily. The thought that we might be leaving for Turpan seemed to please her.

"Do you think it would be possible for your director to call the CITS office in Turpan and ask if a car could be arranged?"

This proposal was enthusiastically adopted by the director.

"Now you must have itinerary for Dunhuang," the pretty girl said. "Dunhuang is an oasis in a sea of sand. There are large sand mountains call dunes and the famous Magao Grotto caves where famous Chinese artifacts are rob by theft from West and . . ."

In March of 1907, Aurel Stein retreated from a fierce sandstorm, what was known around the Takla Makan as a "black hurricane," to the comfort of Dunhuang. Stein categorized himself as "an archaeological explorer"; Owen Lattimore called him "the most prodigious combination of scholar, explorer, archaeologist and geographer of his generation." That he was also a spy for the British secret service seems certain.

He was Jewish, five feet four inches tall, and had an

ability to endure natural hazards that he didn't learn at Oxford and the universities of Vienna and Leipzig.

Because of competing German and Japanese archaeological teams, Stein was anxious to leave Dunhuang and continue excavating the nearby line of watchtowers he had recently discovered and believed (correctly) to be a lost extension of the Great Wall. But in Dunhuang he heard a rumor that a Taoist priest who lived at the nearby sacred caves was guarding a massive hoard of ancient manuscripts.

Wang Yuan-lu was the name of the Taoist priest, and he appears to have been an endearing if bumbling sort of zealot. "He looked a very queer person, extremely shy and nervous," Stein wrote, "with an occasional expression of cunning which was far from encouraging. It was clear from the first that he would be a difficult person to handle."

Abbot—as Stein called him—Wang had stumbled across the cache of manuscripts hidden in a secret chamber while on a pilgrimage to the sacred caves. Deciding this was a divine sign, he appointed himself guardian of the scrolls, securing them behind a locked door to which only he had the key.

But the illiterate Abbot's primary interest was a gaudy restoration of one of the cave sanctuaries in honor of the Buddhist saint Hsuan-tsang. Elaborating on his own admiration of Hsuan-tsang, Stein quickly struck a rapport with the monk. The gold that Stein offered as a contribution to the building efforts did not seem to hurt their relationship as well. Though concerned that the local authorities would not approve, Abbot Wang allowed Stein to enter the locked sanctum of manuscripts.

In a scene that has been compared to the opening of King Tut's tomb, Stein discovered "a solid mass of manuscript bundles rising to a height of nearly ten feet, and filling, as subsequent measurement showed, close on 500 cubic feet."

Over the next several weeks, Stein explored his find slowly, hindered by the Abbot's concern for secrecy. One by one, the Abbot smuggled scrolls from the chamber to Stein. They included not only manuscripts in Chinese, Sanskrit, Sogdian, Tibetan, Runic-Turki, and Uighur but also Buddhist silk paintings, some on banners long enough to hang from the face of the high river cliffs riddled with caves.

In his account, Stein freely admits the Abbot had "been gradually led from one concession to another, and we took care not to leave him much time for reflection." When he left Dunhuang, Stein carried with him twenty-four cases of manuscripts and five of paintings destined for the British Museum. The haul was such that it would take fifty years to catalogue the contents.

One of the cases, it was later discovered, contained the *Diamond Sutra,* printed in 868, the world's earliest printed book. It is displayed in the British Museum next to the Gutenberg Bible.

Six months after Stein left, a French Orientalist, Paul Pelliot, paid a visit to Abbot Wang. He also ingratiated himself with the Abbot and spent a month examining the manuscripts, selecting the most valuable. "On one evening," Pelliot's traveling companion later wrote, "he showed us a Nestorian Gospel of St. John; on another a description, dating from the year 800, of the curious little lake . . . situated in the high dunes south of Tun-wung; another time it was the monastery accounts." For about two hundred dollars Pelliot carried his prize selections back to Paris.

Others followed, and soon it wasn't just the manuscripts they wanted but frescoes from the cave walls as well. With hacksaws and chemical solutions, 1,000-year-old paintings were deported to institutions like the Fogg Museum in Boston.

But all this ended about the time Fleming and Maillart crossed China. A rising nationalism, combined with the humiliation caused by Orientalists on three continents gloating over their booty, set the mood for the creation of a National Council for the Preservation of Chinese Antiquities in Beijing. Eventually, the caves were closed to non-Chinese; few foreigners were allowed to see the caves after "liberation" in 1949; but this stopped completely during the initial frenzy of the Cultural Revolution. Later, when it would have been politically acceptable to admit non-Chinese, authorities continued the ban—to hide the severe damage done to the artwork by the Red Guard.

"But now many, many caves are open," the pleasant CITS girl told us.

"How many?"

"It is difficult to say. They close and open for work."

"Yes, but about how many?"

"Ten, I think."

"But this guidebook says there are 469 caves."

"How could you see so many? Ten is enough, I think."

A good asphalt road covered the 24 kilometers through the desert from Dunhuang to the caves. We wanted to ride bicycles.

"Hotel across the street has bicycles. Many, many bicycles."

She was right. In front of the three-story modern hotel, closed for the winter, we found a bike stand with at least fifty bicycles.

We tried them all. Only two worked.

"Why don't you fix these?" I asked the fellow in charge of the bikes.

"They are very old," he answered. He was in his mid-twenties and rubbed a white lotion continually on his hands.

"I know they're old," I told him. "That's why they need fixing."

"But next year we get new bicycles."

"These are fine if you fix them. But if they don't work, why do you have them for rent?"

"Regulations. Director thinks foreign guests like bicycles very much. It is good service."

"But not if they don't work!"

"Next year, we get new bikes."

We took a taxi.

There was a late fall feeling in the air when we arrived at the caves. Rows of poplar trees shivered in the wind; dried leaves crackled underfoot.

An attractive woman in a bright orange parka was our official guide. She was funny and charming, delivering her memorized spiels with apparent enjoyment. When I asked her why so many of the faces of the Buddhist wall paintings were defaced, she answered with a perfectly straight face, "Weather."

"But isn't it odd that only the faces were affected by the weather?"

"No, not for Chinese weather," she replied. "You would have to be Chinese to understand."

"Of course."

The next morning at the CITS office, I was surprised to find not the girl we had seen the day before or the director but instead the man who had been minding the bicycles. He stood behind the desk reading the *People's Daily;* in his tweed jacket and scarf, he looked like a college student. A plastic bottle of lotion sat on the desk.

He smiled broadly when I came in.

"How are the bicycles?" I asked.

He frowned in a friendly way. "I am guide. The bicycles are a different work unit." He giggled. "I tried to ride bicycle. You are right. They are very bad."

"Why don't you get them fixed?" Like every Chinese town I'd seen, Dunhuang had sidewalk bike repair entrepreneurs who looked competent.

"It is different work unit. I am guide. I speak English."

"What do you do when there are no people to guide?" I knew the caves closed during January and February.

"I study. Like today."

"Is the director in?" I asked.

"He has meeting."

"I wanted to find out if he had talked to the Turpan CITS office."

"Oh, yes. He talk to Turpan. Bad news, I think. In Turpan they say you cannot arrange your itinerary."

"Why not?"

"The roads are blown over. It is not possible. But there is a bus you can take."

"But if the roads are blown over, how can a bus travel on the road?"

"The road is closed to foreigners."

"But I thought it was windblown?"

"Only for foreigners, I think."

All of this was delivered with great sincerity, like the girl who told us the Buddhas were defaced naturally.

I nodded and left. The guide followed me.

"I study English but I never go to America."

We walked outside. The loudspeakers blasted a harsh military anthem.

162

"What is the name of that song?" I asked.

"This?" He listened for a moment, cleaning his glasses on his scarf. "Good News For The Four Modernizations," he said.

"Do you know what the Four Modernizations are?"

"Of course," he answered automatically, stiffening slightly.

When I didn't press him further, he relaxed a bit and asked me, "Is it true in America children do not love their parents?"

"Some do. Probably most, I suppose."

"China is a very poor country but we are rich in spirit, I think."

"Why do you say that?"

He seem surprised at the question. "I think it is true," he said eventually.

"But why do *you* think it's true?"

"I read about America."

"In Political Study Class?"

He nodded. "We all learn English now."

"Is your father a cadre?" I asked. He had the well-kept, educated look of second-generation cadre.

He nodded proudly.

"Does he know English?"

"No. Russian."

Back at the hotel, I found Mark practicing wushu in an empty conference room.

"Bad luck," he said, panting slightly. "I saw the CITS director and he told me he tried to call Turpan but the phones were out."

"He didn't get through?"

"Meo. Impossible to do. So we don't know anything."

We left for Turpan that afternoon.

Chapter Nineteen

It is impossible—in a vague way—to take a train from Dunhuang to Turpan. There is no train station in either town but by traveling two hours by car across the desert you can reach the main Ürümqi-to-Lanchow train line.

The train stop nearest Dunhuang is a tiny place called Liuyuan. Sand blew everywhere into everything. The one restaurant had no rice, eggs, or meat, only dumplings stuffed with a suspicious pork. While David watched the luggage in the station, Mark, Fran, and I hovered over the stove in the restaurant, reluctantly eating the jiaoza. It was 11 degrees.

At a small shop down the street, we bought two dozen Chinese chocolate bars. When I first tasted the Chinese chocolate in Beijing, I thought it terribly bland, with a texture like laminated cardboard. As we traveled farther west and the food grew worse, I was amazed how the taste of the little bars in their aquamarine wrappers improved.

All the windows in Liuyuan were barred. There was a restless, ugly mood in the station; a pair of tough-looking teenagers eyed our baggage—and Fran—with open interest. Smiling, David strolled up to them and offered his hand. He'd grown a beard since arriving in China and his appearance had acquired a certain hard edge. He radiated a tangible sense of frustration as the delays and official mendacity increased. Unlike me, he never complained, but his eyes grew a little wilder at each new twist of Chinese bureaucracy.

The startled punks shook hands with him and moved away.

Despite the cold, a rancid, sour smell permeated the station. I walked outside, feeling queasy.

I found the men's public toilet on the left side of the station. It was the usual brick shell over a concrete trench filled with stalagmites of frozen shit. Just outside the entrance, I saw a cluster of fat dead rats, scattered in a circle as if felled by a grenade. Standing over the trench, a hot rush of vomit shot up my throat.

Afterward, feeling better, I used a mass of Mao notes to clean my hands and face, letting the soiled and crumpled pieces of paper float down onto the piles of waste. I wondered if the shit collectors would find them on their next pick-up and hoped, in a vague way, they would.

It was an overnight train ride to Daheyon, the town nearest Turpan on the rail line. We had tried to book sleeping berths but were told it was impossible. The train began in Lanchow and only at the starting point of a journey could one book a seat.

"But can't you call Lanchow," I'd asked the CITS guide, "and tell them that we've paid you for the berths and they should be reserved."

He cast a long gaze at the telephone sitting ponderously on the desk.

I let the issue drop.

The only way to avoid standing up all night—all the seats were taken—was to persuade a conductor to sell us berths after we boarded the train. This presented two problems. First, there had to be beds free, and secondly, the conductor had to agree to sell the berths. We'd heard from other travelers many horror stories about tyrannical conductors who refused to sell empty bunks to foreigners.

In most countries this problem could be solved with a minor bribe. But in China it was difficult to know if someone would be offended by the offer of some under-the-table kuai. Though there were times when exorbitant sums were requested—the food at the Xinning Binguan, the van rental—all the time I was in China, I never felt that the money was being pocketed by the individual, or at least not the individual who was asking for the money. Of course not knowing if you could depend on a bribe made little problems like getting a bed all the more anxious.

When the train stopped, there was more than the usual nasty pushing among the new passengers. The urgency to leave Liuyuan was extreme. Everyone rushed the narrow entrance to the track at once; it was guarded by a turnstile, which made the transportation of the inevitable hoards of luggage an acrobatic feat. Two old women with red armbands demanded to see the tickets and travel documents of everyone entering the platform. The documents were proof of permission to travel from an individual's work unit. In theory, this was a requirement for travel anywhere in China, but out west it seemed to be enforced more stringently.

All of this took a long time. We had no idea how long the train was supposed to stop in the station. When we reached the platform, an army of blue uniformed women appeared and washed down the dust-caked sides of the train with long-handled mops. Mark hurried onto the train to search for a conductor who would let us "buy up" hard or soft sleepers.

Waiting on the platform, David, Fran, and I plotted our strategy for boarding quickly if the train started to move.

A large, friendly PLA soldier appeared beside us and started to carry our bags onto the train. We resisted, explaining that we were waiting for a friend. I felt like a little old lady being helped across a street I didn't want to cross.

Mark leaned out of a nearby car and motioned for us to board. A moment later he reappeared looking flustered and motioned us back to the platform. This happened several times. At each move we were assisted by the PLA soldier, who developed a most perplexed look.

Eventually Mark triumphed: we got our soft-sleeper berths. The on-and-off, he explained, had been the result of a lively discussion between two conductors as to the availability of berths. One of the conductors had argued that all the berths were taken.

The standard train music, a style that I had come to think of as Chinese martial disco, blared out of a loud-speaker. Normally an advantage of soft-sleeper cars was the inclusion of a volume switch to the PA system, an option not offered in hard seat. But in our car the volume switch was broken. The thought of martial disco at all hours was unbearable, so David climbed up onto the top bunk, unscrewed the twin speakers and disconnected them.

Later, walking to the dining car, I realized that of the seven soft-sleeper compartments, only one other was occupied.

We'd been in Turpan for only a few hours when David announced his intention to leave. He wanted to leave that night, if possible. For good, back to Beijing.

I couldn't really blame him. It hadn't been the best of mornings.

The train had dumped us out at 6:30 A.M. in Daheyon. For some inexplicable reason, we arrived twenty minutes early and had to scramble madly to gather all our gear and hustle off the train before it departed for Ürümqi.

With bags half-stuffed and dropping bits of clothes, we stumbled into the station at Daheyon.

It was pitch black and would remain so until dawn, around 10:00 A.M. Turpan was an hour away by bus. One bus left in the morning, another in the late afternoon. The morning bus left each day fifteen minutes before the train arrived.

We needed to find some kind of vehicle—car, truck, or cart—to take us across the desert to Turpan. Or resolve ourselves to spending the day in Daheyon; even in the dark, it was clear the latter was not a desirable choice.

For several hours we wandered the streets of Daheyon, begging the driver of each vehicle we found to take us to Turpan. None were interested. Eventually we found a post office with a telephone. It was a stand-up model with an earpiece that hooked onto the post. A tough woman postmaster placed the call to the Turpan CITS office, and when they balked at coming to get us, she unleashed a terrifying string of threats. "These are foreign visitors. What is your job if you don't help foreign visitors. Are you too busy to do your job!"

It was very gratifying. While waiting for the car, the postmistress let us sit in a corner of the post office, the only warm place in Daheyon. Mark slept, Fran read Spalding Gray's *Sex and Death to the Age 14*, David went outside to do pushups.

No one was sorry to leave.

I liked Turpan more than any place I'd been in China. It satisfied all my fantasies of oasis life: a sleepy town of mud houses, brightly colored mosques, veiled women, and the best melons in the world.

It was also, clearly, a town under occupation by foreign troops.

Driving into town, our car was stopped by a Han PLA officer; behind him troops blocked the street, goose-stepping toward a barracks. The troops were young; many had soft, boyish features. They carried carbines while their officers shouldered the Chinese version of the AK 47 assault rifle. All were Han.

Veiled Uighur women with young children watched the troops. Our driver, a Uighur, stared blankly.

The Beijing government lists Uighurs as one of China's official fifty-five minorities. As the *Lonely Planet Guide* to China notes in its characteristically blunt manner, "the Uighurs just don't have *anything* in common with the Chinese. The Uighur religion is monotheic Islam, their written script is Arabic, their language is closely related to Turkish, their physical features are basically Caucasian and many could easily be mistaken for Greeks, southern Italians or other southern Europeans."

In 1953, the total population of Xinjiang province was 4.9 million; 3.6 million were Uighur and the rest were a mix of Kazakh and Kirghiz nomads with a fair number of White Russians and their descendants who had slipped over the border after the 1918 revolution. Han Chinese were a distinct minority.

By 1970, there were four million Hans. The 1982 census determined that Xinjiang had a population of thirteen million—only six million were Uighur.

Article fifty of the Chinese People's Political Consultative Conference of 1949 states that "all nationalities in the People's Republic of China are equal. They use unity and mutual aid as weapons to fight against imperialism and the people's public enemies inside all nationalities, to enable the People's Republic of China to become a large affectionate and cooperative family of all nationalities."

When the last of the troops had passed, the Han officer stared at us for a long moment then, with a quick flick of his white glove, allowed our driver to continue to the hotel.

Not so very long ago, the Turpan Guest House was a *caravansari*—a word that crops up frequently in Maillart's and Fleming's books. It's a place where caravans stopped for the night, sort of a camel motel. Its function dictated that there be a large open courtyard for the animals surrounded by rooms for the humans. According to Fleming and Maillart, the animals usually had the better end of the bargain.

"Modernizations"—always a troubling phrase in China—had added various other structures to the Turpan Guest House, including a two-story building topped with an onion-shaped turret next to the main courtyard. It was a confusing, fantastical place.

We were anxious to go to the CITS office to arrange the rest of our journey along the southern rim of the Takla Makan desert. Since leaving Beijing, we had been told that only in Xinjiang province would it be possible to make arrangements to travel on the southern route.

"We must have a meeting," the Turpan CITS director announced after she heard our request.

"A meeting?" I said in a hollow voice, trying to keep my smile in place. Since arriving in China, the word "meeting" had taken on a connotation for me similar to gang rape or torture.

"But if you are head of the CITS office, who else would we need to meet with?" I asked with forced gaiety.

"Many, many people." She became quite solemn.

"The Car Brigade captain. The Public Security Bureau Director. The Head Driver."

"The Head Driver is different than the Car Brigade Captain?" I asked.

She looked at me curiously.

"Of course. How could Head Driver and Car Brigade Captain be same people?"

"My mistake."

The Turpan CITS office was in one of the rooms facing the main square of the Guest House. It was filled mostly with young, attractive Uighur girls, part of the CITS guide force. The Uighur women were a delight— they actually wore skirts (always over thick opaque tights, usually gold or blue) with brightly colored scarves and high-heeled boots. The boots were mostly tall and white, like sixties' "go-go" boots.

Style. That was it. Uighur women hadn't accepted that the democratic tyranny of the proletariat demanded everyone look like soldiers after a tough campaign.

A middle-aged Han woman ran the CITS office. When we came into the office, she was directing a team of workers applying COMPLIMENTS OF TURPAN CITS OFFICE stickers in English, Arabic, and Chinese on a stack of handsome calendars featuring scenes from Xinjiang province. The office had the feel of a high school homeroom before a big pep rally.

"When do you think we could have this meeting?" I asked.

"Oh, we are very busy now. Important work. Next week, I think, maybe."

"What if we go and talk to the Car Brigade leader ourselves."

"He has important meeting."

"More calendars?"

171

"Oh, no. Calendars all done by this office. Very important."

"That's it," David said when we were back outside the office. "I'm sorry, but I just can't do this. Not this waiting around. I'm leaving . . ."

We headed glumly into the dining room for lunch. The dining room was not behind the large doors marked DINING ROOM. It was in a different row of rooms on the main courtyard, entered through a door with a sign reading EXCURSIONS.

There were two adjacent rooms. The first was filled with Uighurs, the second with Han army officers. At a large circular table with empty chairs sat several Japanese. The Uighur hostess steered us to this table; as we approached, the five young men, as if on command, stood and nervously smiled, nodding their heads in a slight bow.

This civility was startling. We shook hands and introduced ourselves.

To my surprise, none of the Japanese spoke English very well. They were dressed in stylish designer outdoor gear—Patagonia jackets and Royal Robbins plaid shirts. Their leader was a handsome fellow with one pierced ear. All carried their own chopsticks in neat boxes that resembled miniature versions of the cue cases used by pool hustlers.

In our depressed state, we were not talkative. The Japanese kept trying different conversation openers along the lines of, "China, interesting, you think?" Our vague nods would set off a flurry of extravagant smiles and head wagging. They would wait for us to say something in response; when we didn't, they would smile harder. It was rather tedious.

Finally, Fran asked what they were doing in Turpan.

"Uighur I photograph," the leader said, holding his hands in a box shape and clicking his tongue.

We all nodded.

"I take picture Uighur. You know Uighur?"

We nodded again.

"In morning, each morning, I travel in bazaar or go out—" he gestured widely, "to fields outside to see people."

"How do you get around?" I asked, wondering if he might have gotten to be friends with the Car Brigade leader. I was desperate for any leads.

He smiled very broadly. "Donkey taxi!" he proclaimed, waving his lacquered chopstick dramatically.

David was adamant about leaving. He had decided to take the train back to Beijing. It was a four- or five-day trip and there were no assurances he wouldn't have to stand all the way.

"But at least I'll be going someplace," he said glumly.

I felt like I was at a funeral. Mark wrote out little scripts that might help David on his trip.

"What does this say?" David asked when Mark handed him an index card with a few lines of Chinese.

"Please help me 'buy up' from hard seat to sleeping berth. I am very tired and need a bed badly. I do not know any Chinese but love China very much."

"Oh."

Fran suggested writing something along the lines of, "I am a crazy American and if I do not get enough sleep I run amok killing Chinese with my bare hands."

I thought it was sure to get results, especially for somebody who looked like David.

"I've got one last idea," Mark said.

I thought he was going to suggest that David wear sunglasses and carry a cane. Pathos seemed to be the desired effect.

"I've got these cards," he said, pulling out of his wallet two impressive business cards with one side printed in English and the other Chinese. They looked quite formal.

Mark explained that they were given to him by attachés of the Chinese consulate in New York. He had met them when he had received a frantic call for help from a Chinese martial arts troupe visiting New York, who had brought a translator from China who spoke only Spanish.

I suggested trying to call the attachés in New York to use their influence to secure our elusive travel permission.

"Call? America?" David interrupted his packing to look at me in astonishment. "From Turpan?"

These were my friends. No one laughed too loudly.

It was decided the cards should be employed in a grand bluff with the CITS office. I volunteered to do battle. David continued to pack, and Fran helped Mark with his instant traveler's phrases.

"How about 'Please don't spit on my shoes?' " she suggested.

The calendar party was still in full swing when I returned to the CITS office.

I requested a meeting with the manager, who sat on the floor working over a stack of calendars. She rose, fixed me with a serious look, and sat on the edge of the cot in the office. There were actually three cots in the office. I sat on another.

In a formal manner, I presented the cards. "I could not say this before because it embarrasses him, but my friend is a very famous American scholar and a great friend of China. He is touring China at the request of these very important men from the Chinese consulate in New York City in America. He is writing a book about CITS and how conditions have changed for the foreign visitor in China . . ."

I went on in this vein for some time. By the end, I believe, I had explained that Mark had been requested by Deng Xiaoping to address the Party Conference in the Great Hall of the People before returning to America.

"You want permission to hire car for itinerary on Silk Road through Hotan?"

I nodded ferociously.

"I must have meeting with Car Brigade Leader."

"Yes, but—"

She spoke quickly to a pot-bellied Han crouched on the floor attaching labels. I'd noticed him before because of the cigar he'd been smoking. I wanted to ask him where I could buy one.

After a short exchange with no visible reaction on his part, she turned to me and said, "The Car Brigade leader says it is possible."

"Yes?"

"But you must have permission of Public Security Bureau."

"Oh."

"They are very nice. It is no problem."

She directed me to the Public Security Bureau. It was across the courtyard of the Turpan Guest House on the second floor.

A sign on the door read "The Post Office is open at 10 in the morning." A hand-drawn sign detailed the route to the Turpan post office. The door was locked, and no one was inside.

I went back to the CITS office.

"Is that the right office?" I asked, pointing across the courtyard.

"Yes."

"But there's no sign that says Public Security, and there's some notice on the door about the Turpan Post Office."

"Yes," she nodded.

"And no one is there," I added.

"Yes," she said. "The officer is never in now."

"Then how will I talk to him?"

"That is problem. You stay here?"

I nodded.

"I tell him to come to your room."

"But how will you see him if he is never in?"

"We are very busy!" she snapped at me.

"I think we should call New York and talk to our friends. They can explain how important this is."

She looked at me with a puzzled look, as if trying to judge if I was serious. I waved Mark's cards. "The numbers are on here." I moved toward the phone.

"What is your room number?" she asked. Her large tortoiseshell glasses slipped down her nose. She pushed them up with the back of her hand.

I told her.

"I talk to him," she said, nodding.

Back at the room, Fran cut Mark's hair while David repeated the phrases Mark had written out for him. He sounded like a country music singer ordering from a Chinese menu.

"Well?" Mark asked.

I started to explain what had happened but gave up after a few sentences. David reiterated his conviction that he would leave on the night train.

A throaty roar vibrated from the bathroom followed by loud clanging and then a high-pitched squeal.

"Ah-hah!" Fran dashed hopefully into the bathroom. She emerged downcast.

"No water," David said when he noticed my confused look. "We turned all the taps on full just in case it changes its mind."

"It?" I asked.

"The Chinese water god," Fran said, settling down beside Mark to finish his spiked haircut.

Chapter Twenty

W u Tong-Guang, the Turpan Public Security Bureau chief, was a short, handsome Han dressed in young executive style: gray slacks and blue V-neck sweater. I was astonished when he actually appeared at our door. That he seemed genuinely interested in helping us seemed like a miracle.

He knocked on the door just as Fran finished Mark's haircut. Mark, bare-chested, sat in a chair with Fran behind him. She had cut almost all the hair off the sides of his head, leaving a shock on the top standing straight up.

As I went to the door, it occurred to me that it was the first time anyone had knocked on a door since I'd been in China. The custom, apparently, was simply to walk straight in.

Wu Tong-Guang seemed only slightly surprised by the scene he'd stumbled into. Mark greeted him with great aplomb. I rushed to offer him a Marlboro. He declined.

I spread the map out and explained where we wanted to go. Wu Tong-Guang was intrigued by the English names on our map. He pointed to Taiwan and asked innocently what was the name of the island.

"Taiwan province," Mark asserted.

Wu Tong-Guang beamed at hearing the official government name for the island his country covets.

We talked for over an hour. At the end, Wu Tong-Guang stood up and announced he had "to make a report" to his superiors in Ürümqi. He indicated the pad of notes he had taken.

Ürümqi was a day's ride north of Turpan.

"Does that mean you have to go to Ürümqi?" Mark asked with transparent cheer.

Of course not, Wu Tong-Guang countered, as if the idea were preposterous. He would call them on the telephone.

I wasn't sure if this was good or bad.

As far as he was concerned, Wu Tong-Guang said as he left, our plan was fine. He must check with his superiors but there should be no problem.

All of this put David in a quandary. If we were granted permission to take the southern route, he didn't want to leave. But if we were delayed for days waiting for an answer, then he wanted to escape on the night train. It was all a guess.

In the end, he elected to stay.

An hour later, he was glad he did.

Wu Tong-Guang reappeared, breaking all records for Chinese bureaucracy. As far as the Public Security Bureau was concerned, it was fine for us to hire a CITS car for the southern route.

It was a moment of some joy in Turpan.

We ate in the market that night. The free market in Turpan was the largest, most vigorous I'd seen in China, row after row of stands attended by Uighurs who flamboyantly hawked their goods. They wore round skullcaps circled with bands of fur and tall boots made of hardened felt. At a boot stand, Mark and I tried, with little success, to learn what process was employed to stiffen the felt. Also, I asked if it would be possible to have a pair made for my size twelve feet. The boots had no soles or treads other than the rounded felt; the Uighurs who wore them walked with a curious sway, as if they were crossing a pitching deck in a moderate storm. The boots were reputed to be very warm, though what made them such eluded explanation.

We ate noodles with shards of mutton and hot pepper for dinner. The preparation was an elaborate process. On a thick piece of wood, dough was flattened by a young Uigher girl; her older sister stretched the dough into noodles with an exaggerated accordion motion, swinging her arms theatrically. Their mother did the actual cooking, first frying the bright red hunks of lamb in deep oil at the bottom of a soot-blackened wok, then adding the noodles, onions, and peppers.

There was a whole section of the market dedicated to noodle stands. The chefs stood beside their coal-burning stoves yelling and touting their noodles. Behind the cooking area, each of the stalls had rows of long benches, like a Turkistan version of a German beer garden. Modern tape players serenaded diners with high-pitched music.

Turpan in early evening was a place of sharp, surprising images. The sun setting over the desert threw a golden haze over the dusty streets and alleys. Wild-looking Muslim children played in the dirt, striking homemade tops with rough whips. Irrigation canals lined the streets.

Off the main streets, away from the Han troops and the revolutionary statue at the city center, it was quite easy to forget that you were in China. The blue-eyed Muslim men and women didn't wear Mao suits or surgical masks, and didn't spit on the street.

This was a feeling that lasted exactly as long as you could delay dealing with the other China, the official

China of permission and reports; the China of CITS and Public Security bureaus.

"We would like very much to arrange your itinerary," the CITS manager told me when I arrived in her office to make arrangements. "But there is a problem with fuel."

"What kind of problem?"

"There is none on road."

I pulled out my worn map. "You mean all along this road," I traced the loop around the Takla Makan, "there is no gas?"

She nodded, seemingly relieved that I had understood so quickly.

"But how do people get from one town to another?"

"Bicycles. Many bicycles in China."

"They bicycle across hundreds of kilometers of desert? And how do they get food and medicine? Here in Hotan," I pointed to the town at the bottom of the desert road, "they make carpets famous all over the world. How do they get those carpets out of Hotan? On a bicycle?"

"Oh, no. Trucks. Trucks, of course."

"But if there's gas for trucks, why isn't there gas for your jeeps?" I pointed toward the new Japanese jeeps parked out front.

"Different kind of gas," she said quickly, "for trucks and jeeps."

"You mean diesel? But you have diesel jeeps."

"But they are Japanese diesel. The trucks are Chinese. Japanese and Chinese use different kind of diesel."

What struck me as so odd about this encounter was that I knew this woman was intelligent. And educated.

David left that afternoon. Mark went with him in the taxi on the hour-long trip across the desert to Daheyon. He returned looking heartbroken.

"It was a nightmare. I left him standing beside the tracks with his handful of phrases. The station was jammed. It's five nights to Beijing . . ."

I was in no hurry to leave Turpan. Each morning I woke up to the sound of braying donkeys—there were many donkeys in Turpan—and had breakfast in the EXCURSIONS room. Uighurs like coffee, and the EXCURSIONS room offered the best I'd had in China, along with twists of fried dough. Afterward, I would walk around town while the sun rose. This happened around ten o'-clock. . . .

Each morning the rising sun burned away the thick ground fog, gradually revealing a series of dramatic images: the veiled woman hurrying into a walled entrance way; the minarets of the mosque floating disembodied atop the sea of fog; a stream of donkey carts loaded with sugarcane heading to the bazaar. And always there were the old men with spiked gray beards, arms folded into their coats, leaning against mud walls. They struck me, without exception, as angry.

The men were a reminder that, though it looked peaceful enough, Turpan had a past of celebrated violence. When Dr. Albert Regal, a Russian botanist/spy, escaped from house arrest in Turpan in 1879, his guards were executed according to local custom described in *Foreign Devils on the Silk Road*:

> The victim was incarcerated in a specially built cage known as a *kapas*. His head, firmly secured, stuck out of the top, while his feet rested on a board. The latter was gradually

lowered, day by day, until on about the eighth day his neck finally broke.

"Civil death" was another form of ritualistic execution in Turpan. "The offender was taken out with various ceremonies on a sunny day and placed against a tree," Jack Chin describes in *The Sinkiang Story*. "His shadow cast on the tree was marked out in outline. He was then confined to his house and from then on his relatives were obliged to consider him dead as of that date."

In the bazaar one morning, I met Ai Nijang. He was a Uighur, twenty-eight, and worked as a combination nurse and orderly in the Uighur Turpan hospital. The Hans, he explained, had their own hospital.

Ai Nijang was tall and good-looking; he dressed with the neatness of an English banker and had a gentle smile that stayed with him even when we talked about the most unpleasant of topics, like what had happened to Turpan in the Cultural Revolution and how much his friends hated the Han troops.

"Me," he said, "I never make fight. I work in my job and my boss is a Han. I like him. During Cultural Revolution he was made to wear a funny hat, how do you call it . . ." he shaped a funnel on top of his head.

A dunce cap, I told him.

He nodded, laughing ruefully at the image. "This is famous doctor. And in his funny hat, he must march around and around Shanghai, like Long March. You know Long March?"

"Of course. One of the great Helmsman's finest hours."

We laughed.

I took long walks through Turpan with Ai Nijang. He was popular, greeted often by his friends. On the way to the post office one afternoon, we were stopped by a young man, obviously a good friend, who looked Han.

"That is the first friend of yours I've met who was Han," I said after the two had discussed an upcoming marriage.

"No, he is not Chinese. He is Hui."

Ai Nijang explained that the Hui were Muslim, like the Uighur.

"Can you tell the difference between Hui and Han."

"Of course."

"But how."

"Many wear the little white hats." He pointed to an old man wearing a Muslim skullcap.

"Yes, but your friend didn't. He looked just like a Han to me."

"There is a difference. And why do you say 'Han' not 'Chinese'?"

"Aren't Chinese anyone who lives in China?"

"They are Chinese, we are Uighur."

"But the Uighur live in China."

"Not all Uighur. Some live in Soviet country."

"Russia? How many?"

"Many, I think. Many Uighur move to Soviet in Cultural Revolution."

"Did Uighurs leave Turpan?"

He nodded. "I wish they go to your country."

"Why?"

"Then I have relatives in your country. Then maybe I can get passport."

"There are many Chinese in America."

He smiled. "But not Uighur! You understand."

"Would you like a passport?"

It was, I instantly realized, a cruel question. Ai Nijang gave me a plaintive but bemused look.

"What if Fran said she was your relative?" Ai Nijang

184

had commented that Fran's features had a Uighur cast.

"There is better way."

"What?"

"I marry her. That is better, I think."

Ai Nijang wanted me to see the Uighur museum at the center of town. "Turpan is an important town in Uighur history," he said.

"What's in the museum?"

"Many old things." He paused. "Relics."

"Uighur relics?"

"Yes!"

Each time we went to the museum it was closed, despite a prominent sign claiming it was open eight hours a day.

"Very irregular," Ai Nijang said.

Ai Nijang also wanted to take me to a school where a cousin was a teacher. There were separate Uighur and Han schools, he explained. The schools used to be very bad but now they are better.

"Why?"

"I show you," he promised, grinning proudly.

The school was a walled compound not unlike the one in Golmud, but many of the mud walls were decorated with bright murals. Most showed Han and Uighur children playing together in idyllic oasis conditions.

Ai Nijang's cousin was not at school. "Political study meeting," he explained. "It is Wednesday afternoon, I forget. Always political study meeting on Wednesday afternoon."

"What happens at political study?"

"It is very boring. People sit in a circle and talk. A Little Group Leader leads the discussion."

"Do you go."

He nodded. "I read the paper." He shrugged.

"The *People's Daily*?"

"Of course! I am good Party member!"

"Ai Nijang," I asked, "tell me why the schools are better now than before."

He smiled. "Now the children have some classes in Uighur."

"Do they have to learn Chinese?"

"Yes, of course."

"And do the Chinese have to learn Uighur?"

"Not yet," he answered with a teasing glint. "Maybe later we make them."

Our Japanese dinner partners were very taken with Fran. The competition among them to impress her grew fierce in the polite, understated way the Japanese have adopted as their post-war manner.

The photographer talked about his work. He was in Turpan for a month shooting black and white portraits of Uighers. He worked as a commercial photographer back in Tokyo but hoped this would help him make a transition. "I want to be artist," he said, gesturing dramatically with his chopsticks. "This what I want my life."

He left each morning by donkey taxi to find new subjects. I asked how much the donkey taxis cost.

"It matters how fast you go. One kuai, like this . . ." Using his fingers to imitate donkey legs, he crept his hand across the table.

"Two kuai . . ." His fingers picked up speed.

"Three kuai . . ." Faster.

"Four kuai . . ." His fingers raced across the table, knocking over a bottle of Five Star beer. Everyone roared.

The Japanese had seen Fran jogging and were greatly impressed. Several times they commented to me in a low voice, as if it were a dark sexual secret, about how strong Fran looked.

"Yes," I finally said, "she is a famous American woman fighter."

Their eyes widened.

"Like Muhammad Ali. Woman boxer. Here in China she studies martial arts with masters."

"Fight men or women?"

"Women professionally," I said reassuringly. "That is how the sport is." We all nodded together sagely. "But she loves to fight men for fun."

From then on, their pursuit of Fran grew more heated.

There was, theoretically at least, one remaining hope of traveling on the southern route legally. The Turpan CITS manager assured me that if we went to Ürümqi, the CITS office there could make arrangements.

"They can do this, I know. You should take train to Ürümqi."

"But you told me the problem was with fuel. If there isn't gas—the right gas, that is—how can going to another office change anything."

"Oh, they can change anything."

I was tired of this sport. Ai Nijang had confided that the real reason the CITS office didn't want to make the trip was that a driver had been killed in a nasty accident recently in the desert and the other drivers were inclined to stay around home. When I'd mentioned this to the Dragon Lady, she'd bristled and insisted Chinese drivers will go anyplace.

I spent most of a day trying to call the Ürümqi CITS

office. When I eventually got through, an intelligent female voice immediately embarked on an explanation of how difficult our trip would be—this time because of snow.

"Is there any problem with fuel?"

"Problems? What problems?"

I repeated what the Dragon Lady had told me, though I didn't tell her where I had heard it.

"That is crazy. What problem gas?"

But snow, unfortunately, was a problem and by now I knew enough to understand that if the snow problem was mysteriously alleviated then it would be replaced by the rain problem or the flooding problem or . . .

I just didn't have the stomach for it anymore. All I wanted to do was get to Kashgar, and if that meant going on the northern route, so be it.

"We'll just have to take a bus," Fran said one night over dinner. "It won't be so bad."

That opinion struck me as extremely unwarranted optimism. We knew the bus took at least three days; some people claimed it might take five.

"But it stops at night," Ai Nijang told us cheerfully. "You can sleep. It will be okay, I think."

Chapter
Twenty-One

It was somewhere around mid-morning, when we'd been on the road for four or five hours and the sun was just coming up, that I realized what I was traveling in was not so much a bus but a frozen toilet on wheels.

This thought came to me right after a bump had tossed me out of my seat onto the floor. I landed in a mixture of vomit and baby urine. The young mother across from me looked down sympathetically and offered her tiny hand, a friendly gesture aborted suddenly by another attack of the nausea she'd been struggling with all morning. She leaned sideways and wretched at my feet. We hit another bump and the seat cushions—a generous classification—flew up all around me like pancakes tossed on a griddle.

I remembered, like scenes from another life, the outrage I would routinely express at airport counters whenever forced to take the center seat on a plane. "You don't have an aisle? You really expect me to . . ."

At 6:00 A.M., in the station at Daheyon, the bus hadn't looked so bad. With my increasingly sophisticated eye, I'd noticed immediately that the seats had solid backs, not the hollow kind that guaranteed you'd be riding all day with someone's knees jammed in your back. And though it didn't have heat, it also lacked the branding iron along the baseboard. One less life-threatening obstacle.

There was a tremendous crowd squeezed into the square cement box that served as a station. Mark, Fran, and I elected to wait outside in front of the bus door, braced for the hand-to-hand seating struggle. In one great rush, the crowd poured out of the station—and onto the bus next to ours. After checking that we had the right bus, we were elated. We pulled out of the station with a scraggly group filling only half the seats.

In a celebration of the unexpected room, I stretched out on the back row of seats and tried to sleep. I soon realized it was like trying to doze in a refrigerated washing machine. Not only did the bus lack heat, all the windows were broken or severely cracked. I tried to light a match to read my thermometer but it was impossible in the brisk cross-breeze.

The bus vibrated continuously, interspersed with violent bumps. In the dimness, I watched a baby shoot upward out of his mother's arms to be caught by his father. The little scene had the disastrous potential and happy ending of a well-rehearsed vaudeville act.

I wore: a layer of thin long underwear; another layer of thicker long underwear made from a miracle material called capeline; heavy wool pants; a wool shirt; a down vest; an expedition parka; my PLA flap hat; and ski gloves. My feet were wrapped in two Patagonia synchilla hats in addition to thick socks and boots.

I ran through this list in my head because I was cold and wondered what else I could put on. But I was wearing almost everything I had brought to China.

There was only one thing to do. I pulled out my sleeping bag and crawled in. The young mothers, seeing me in what looked like a giant baby snuggler, looked at me jealously. Even the woman who had been wretching stopped and reached out imploringly, holding out her baby as if she wanted me to slip it inside the bag with me.

I declined.

The sun came up with a primeval, first-dawn quality I had begun to expect in desert China. There was an intimidating line of peaks to the south and brown wasteland ahead. The interior of the bus had been painted green a long time ago; a silly fringe of dirty cloth hung from the ceiling, as if a decorator had once tried to create a romantic surrey feel for the conveyance.

At the very front of the bus, the official team of driver, female conductor, and traveling mechanic rode in a separate compartment divided by a door of broken glass. This little section appeared heated, and there was no vomit or urine on the floor. I viewed it enviously as a first-class haven and wondered what matter of bribe or enticement—I was up for anything—it might take to gain entrance.

The ride to Kashgar from Turpan cost 38 kuai—$10.50. When inquiring at the station how many days the trip would last, we received only the reassurance that however many it did take, the price would be the same. I found this particularly uncomforting.

By noon we were straining over high mountains of snow and ice. My thermometer hovered around 0 degrees, but the wind chill was fierce. The woman in front of me had progressed from wretching to a comatose state that was frighteningly similar to death. I supposed this was in reaction to the altitude, a malady to which people who lived in the Turfan Depression no doubt were especially susceptible.

Around one o'clock we stopped for lunch at a bleak mountain outpost reeking of diesel fuel. A group of Hans played pool on a rough table outside the blockhouse restaurant. The players were in their twenties and wore high-heeled boots and scarves jauntily thrown over their shoulders. The table was a piece of green plywood balanced imperfectly on a pair of sawhorses. It had a hole in each corner but no pockets under the holes; several urchins scrambled for the ball whenever a shot was sunk, scurrying under the table legs with an efficiency worthy of the best ball boys at Wimbledon. The players chewed sunflower seeds and struck exaggerated poses between shots.

The restaurant served a delicious brown noodle in a thick gravy with onions and lamb fat. Outside, I bought some cookies in a rough cardboard box loosely stapled together. The cookies had no taste whatsoever. As an experiment, I broke off a piece of the box and chewed on it. While the textures were slightly different, the taste was indistinguishable.

All afternoon we passed through oasis towns, jumbles of mud huts clinging together for support. Snow covered everything; this was a surprise. Fran said it looked like the Arctic, a desert Arctic, and that captured it well.

The Uighur women all wore brightly colored scarves wrapped mummy-style around their head for warmth. I would have done the same except my scarf had fallen into a pool of vomit.

By late afternoon we had moved from the mountains to a flat, high plain. The road was smoother but icier and more treacherous. We crept along, surging occasionally up to 20 mph. I tried to read *Hindoo Holiday* by J.R. Ackerly in hope that the stories of tropical India would raise my body temperature by sympathetic association. But the bus shook so much reading was a struggle. I gave up and tried to think of Mississippi summers. That worked a little better.

As it began to get dark, we pulled into Korla where we were to stop for the night. Before reaching the inn, however, we stopped at a repair yard. For a long time, the mechanic who'd traveled with us from Turpan banged away under the bus. The yard was full of crumpled buses, obvious relics of hideous collisions. They stood as reminders of previous failed repair jobs.

Finally we pulled away and traveled across town to an inn. On the way the conductress got off and said, "See you at 7:00." But the driver interrupted, asserting we were to leave at 6:00. The conductress nodded and turned around to face the passengers and said, loudly, "Okay, see you at 7:00," then got off.

The inn was in a walled compound surrounded by food stands. Fires flared in the darkness, and donkey carts moved down the dirt street. It all felt medieval.

A Han behind a glass counter dispersed room numbers like a drill sergeant. Everyone lined up to get their room assignment and a battered metal tin of hot water for washing. The place stank of sweat and mold. Behind us in line, the woman who had been vomiting all day on the bus began to vomit on the floor.

"The room is only three yuan," Mark said. "Seventy-five cents."

"Overpriced," I muttered.

"Don't worry," Fran said. "Today was the worst day. I'm sure of it."

Chapter
Twenty-Two

I t was about 10:30 the next morning when the bus broke
down for the first time.

The day had started on a calamitous note. Before
leaving the parking lot, the conductress evicted a half-
dozen people. They had boarded the bus in Korla wanting
to go to Kashgar, but the conductress claimed that this
was a through bus only and no new passengers were
allowed after Turpan. This made little sense as we had
picked up roadside passengers all during the ride from
Turpan. But the conductress held firm.

Then she threw off an old woman dressed in rags
who'd ridden with us from Turpan. The conductress apparently had never collected a ticket from her, and when
the old woman couldn't produce one the second morning,
off she went.

But all of this was just a warm-up for the title bout.
This erupted when the conductress demanded an additional mao—about a nickel—from a well-dressed man
who looked prosperous enough to be a cadre. The argument quickly became a matter of face for each, with
voices rising in the dark bus. Finally the conductress, like
an angry umpire, jerked her thumb toward the door, yelling at the man to get off.

"Are you a thing?" he shouted. "I see a thing, not a

human being. Once they had human beings as bus attendants now I see they only have things!"

The conductress did not take this quietly. She grabbed the man and pulled him toward the door.

This all took a long time. Everyone watched it quietly, trying to stay warm in the freezing darkness. The driver sat impassively, leaning forward sideways in his seat, his chin cupped in his hands.

Rising up in my seat and fumbling with the sleeping bag that I'd wrapped myself in, I took out a handful of money and pushed it toward the man. Everyone on the bus applauded and yelled their approval.

Of course it did no good. It was a matter of face, not money. The man began to push the conductress. I waited for someone to intervene and when they didn't, I jammed myself between the two combatants. The man, though startled, continued to yell loudly. Then the driver joined the fray.

"A mao is a mao but the names you have called this woman cannot be forgiven!"

I was not aware the man had asked for forgiveness.

"I will make a report!" the man shouted, trying to keep one foot on the bus.

"And so will I, comrade! You will never get to Kashgar!"

It was about 8:00 when we finally left the station. The man stood in the parking lot waving his fist and shouting details of his report.

Around 10:30 we stopped to pick up three Muslim men standing beside the road. They were all over six feet tall and wore long dark coats and fur hats. These were intimidating characters. One sat down next to two typically slight Han men who hurried to make room.

While they got on, the driver and mechanic got out, banged around underneath the bus, then lifted the hood. The conductress announced a short break. (With the group bathroom breaks and snack times under the tight rein of the conductress, the journey was beginning to remind me of a school field trip.)

An hour later we boarded. The bus lurched on, and though the road was clear and flat, we never broke twenty miles an hour. Ten mph was the norm.

Fifty minutes later, it stopped again. More banging under the hood, more waiting. The sand along the road was thick and clinging. A five-minute walk had me panting. The road was lined with black scrub trees covered in a brilliant white frost, the sort of trees that belonged in a Christmas pageant.

Christmas. I hadn't thought about it for weeks. It was only three days off.

At lunch, just as I was downing my fourth skewer of delicious grilled lamb, we heard the bad news. We'd stopped at a typical noodle-and-dumpling dive but this one was surrounded by a market with food stands. There was hot flat bread, spicy lamb cooked to order on small charcoal grills, and Turpan melons.

The feast improved my mood considerably, until the driver confided to Mark and me that we weren't going to make it to Kashgar the next day, or perhaps for several days. He wanted us to understand that it was the bus's fault, not his.

This was not very comforting.

We got back on the bus. It was not a happy moment. I had a great pile of flat bread I'd bought at the market and I proceeded to eat all of it, piece by piece, in a compulsive manner. The young mother had fainted again and was sprawled sideways in the aisle. No one seemed to care. I was rapidly developing an antipathy for everyone on the bus.

At mid-afternoon we stopped at a way station in the town of Kucha. Beggars and bums loitered inside the cavernous building. Fran suggested that we find another bus to Kashgar. In theory we knew that there should be other buses passing through here from Ürümqi.

But the woman behind the counter shrugged when Mark asked when the next bus to Kashgar might be stopping.

"There is one here now," she said sullenly.

"Yes, we know. But when will another come through?"

"This bus isn't right for you?"

"We think it is broken. It has engine problems."

She shrugged again. "The next bus may be worse. Why get off this bus for another?"

This seemed reasonable, and Mark agreed. But I am always one to believe there has to be a better way.

"Mark," I said, "let's ask some of the truck drivers out front if they'll take us."

"Are you serious?"

"Let's just ask, it can't hurt."

There was a brightly painted van parked outside the station filled with a mixed group of Hans and Uighers, the first such intermingling I'd seen. All were dressed in the standard garb of Chinese punks—high black boots, sunglasses, jeans. Nearby stood a couple of attractive women with babies.

"You don't want to go to Kashgar," they said when Mark asked about a ride.

"Why?"

"We've just been there."

They reminded me of a roving group of sixties hippies. I wondered how they were able to travel around.

"You didn't like it?"

"There is nothing to do."

That there might be something to "do" in Kashgar had never occurred to me.

"We're going to Ürümqi," one asserted proudly, as if it were Paris.

We went into a big building next to the station. Like the station, it was new but falling apart.

Mark asked a teenager behind a counter about possible rides to Kashgar. He suggested we call the transportation work unit in town. But he didn't have a number. Next to the counter someone shouted into a phone. "Wei! Wei!"

Mark asked him how we might get the number. Was there a phone directory?

He shook his head.

"Wei! Wei!"

"This is hopeless," Mark said, looking exhausted.

"Ask him if the transportation unit is nearby. Maybe we can just go there."

Mark sighed and posed the question.

"He says he isn't sure there *is* such a unit. But there should be if there's not."

We got back on the bus.

The asphalt road soon faded to gravel. We bounced along at ten miles per hour.

At five o'clock the driver surrendered for the day, turning into a walled compound like the one we'd stopped in the night before. We weren't really in a town; it was more like an encampment that had sprung up where the gravel road narrowed and turned sharply right. Since all traffic had to slow down to negotiate this turn, several food stands had been built on both sides of the road to take advantage of the selling opportunities presented by the natural obstacle.

Since several hours of daylight remained, it did not bode well that the driver decided he could go no farther. As soon as we stopped, he and the mechanic donned grimy smocks and began banging under the hood. When we asked for a prognosis, they shrugged and banged harder.

There were many trucks pulled off the road beside the food stalls. I suggested to Mark that we should ask for a ride to Kashgar.

"Just go up and ask these guys?"

"Yes."

"And where are we going to sit?"

That was a problem. Since there were three of us, we had to find a truck with room in the back. Tankers were out.

Reluctantly, Mark circulated among the trucks making inquiries. I accompanied him while Fran remained at the compound watching our luggage. The drivers looked very tough. Their vehicles did not appear to be in much better shape than our dilapidated bus.

"You would really go with one of these guys?" Mark asked, making it sound like something he didn't want to do.

"Sure," I answered blithely. "Why not?"

"Why? Why? Just look at these guys! And look at their trucks! What are you going to do when they break down? Half of them are parked here because they've got problems. At least with the bus, we know we'll eventually make it."

I didn't see any harm in asking, particularly since there wasn't much else to do. I conveyed this in a heated voice.

Both steaming, we returned to the dirty walled compound. A group of at least fifty locals had gathered around Fran. Like the Tibetans, they stared open-mouthed.

We waded through the crowd. A sudden spurt of passing trucks encouraged me.

"What we ought to do," I said, "is to stand out here and flag down anything going by."

Mark glowered, but agreed.

For an hour or so we stood out in the road. A few trucks stopped. Some were not going to Kashgar; others said they couldn't take us because they didn't have room. Two modern vans of the sort CITS used passed but refused to stop. I took out a handful of large FEC bills to wave at the next van. The sight of the FEC drew a renewed crowd; I welcomed the throng because it helped block the road and increased the odds any vehicle would have to stop.

Mark announced he was going to find a room and lie down. He looked miserable.

With renewed vigor, Fran and I waved the FEC and repeated "Aksu, Kashi!" at every vehicle that passed. Aksu was the next large town on the way to Kashgar or Kashi.

This primitive sign language drew several interested parties. One Boy Scout type nodded energetically and made steering motions followed by a pounding of his chest.

"I think he's trying to tell us he can drive," Fran said. She was in a remarkably good mood. "I'll take him around to Mark and see what the story is." She went off toward the inn followed by the Boy Scout and a dozen accomplices.

I stayed out on the road, vainly looking for a willing driver. Fran returned about twenty minutes later. Laughing, she described Mark besieged by the Boy Scout and his group. The discussion was still continuing but it seemed while they were eager to drive, they didn't have a vehicle.

"Details, details," Fran said.

Another group presented itself, three wild-haired young Uighurs and a Han. They wore bits and pieces of some kind of pale green uniform—a coat here, trousers there. The Han spoke a smattering of English.

"You have truck?" I asked, athletically turning my hands in a pantomime of driving.

He nodded, looking confused. "Truck? Yes."

The Han was tall and wore glasses. He seemed quiet and deliberate, the opposite of the Uighers. They jumped up and down nervously, shouting, "Aksu? Aksu!"

The lead Uighur, who wore bulky sunglasses, grabbed my arm and pulled me over to his vehicle. He threw out his hand in a gesture of blatant pride. All that was missing was a drum roll.

It was a big green dump truck, ten or fifteen years old. At the Uighur's insistence, Fran and I climbed aboard. He spun his hat on his head jauntily, and showed us his truck's accessories—lights, horn, windows, windshield wipers, even a cassette player. Grabbing a Talking Heads tape from Fran, he jammed it in. David Byrne rocked the cab. The Uighur smiled broadly, nodding his head in time to "Psycho Killer." He revved the engine then popped it into gear. With a violent lurch, we shot forward, scattering the sizable crowd of onlookers.

"Good!" he cried, pounding the wheel. His companions ran after us.

We pointed him toward the compound where Mark had rented a room. Keeping the truck in low gear, he muscled it over a curb, flying into the dirt courtyard. The bus conductress, on her way to eat at the food stalls, stared at us, shaking her finger in disapproval.

In his narrow room, Mark lay on a cot still surrounded by the Boy Scout and his friends. He groaned when we charged in.

"Aksu! Aksu!"

We dismissed the Boy Scout and his entourage and commenced negotiations with the Uighurs and their Han accomplice. The driver was named Ali; the other Uighur was his brother, Muhammad. The Han's name was Kim.

Ali agreed to drive us to Aksu. Price: three hundred kuai. When Mark explained we really wanted to go to Kashgar, Ali seemed confused.

"But why do you say Aksu if Kashi is your destination?"

Mark pointed out that *he* hadn't said Aksu; Fran and I had said it and we didn't speak Chinese.

"I can take you to Kashi," Ali said. "Yes, but don't worry if I have to take something with us."

"What do you mean?"

Ali told us his truck had to carry meat back to his work unit in Korla. He was on his way to Aksu to buy it, because meat was cheaper there than in Korla. If we wanted to go to Kashgar, he could buy the meat first then take us.

I had visions of riding to Kashgar stacked in with slabs of mutton.

Fran suggested that Ali take us to Kashgar first then return to Aksu to buy meat.

Ali seemed very eager to please Fran. He kept looking up at her and smiling shyly. He moved around the tiny room constantly, standing up, sitting down, pacing.

Suddenly Ali stopped pacing and pointed to Fran. "Kashi? Yes!"

We returned to negotiating the price. This didn't take long as Mark hated to barter, and Fran and I were willing to pay anything not to get back on the bus. We finally agreed on 600 kuai ($140.00), down from 700. It was a fortune by Chinese standards and not an insignificant sum by American. But Ali was very suave.

The money, he explained, meant nothing to him or his brother. In Korla his mother ran a restaurant and made 1,200 kuai a month. They had three television sets and 25,000 kuai saved up.

Mark pointed out we would pay in FEC.

Ali shrugged. He had everything you could buy at the Friendship Store. But what they really wanted was a robot, like in America. If we had a robot—a good robot—they would take that instead of the money.

A robot? What kind of robot?

He thought for a moment. Any kind. An American robot.

Mark tried to explain that Americans didn't really have robots.

Ali would not believe it. He thought we were putting him on. Just because China was a poor country, he insisted, didn't mean he and his brother were stupid. How did the American build his own rocket to the moon if it wasn't with robots?

Rocket to the moon?

Ali had read about it in the *People's Daily*. His brother and Kim confirmed it was true, they had read it as well. An American had built a rocket out of scrap parts and ridden it to the moon and back.

Mark agreed that probably this man did have robots.

I told you! Ali crowed.

We moved the conversation back to traveling to Kashgar. I suggested to Mark that we pay half of the money now and half when we arrived in Kashgar.

Ali was outraged. Are foreigners so untrustworthy that they don't trust anyone else? he said. Here is my work card! Take down my number!

He whipped out a little plastic red folder with his photo identification. Kim and Muhammad did the same when Ali glowered at them.

Still on his cot, Mark stared woefully at the three work cards. "What should I say?" he asked.

Fran and I, properly shamed, agreed to pay the full amount. But Ali snapped shut his work card and declared he didn't want our money now, we could pay in Kashgar if we were happy with the journey.

Everyone shook hands. The deal was set.

As we loaded our gear in his truck, Ali expressed his desire for Mark, Fran, and me to ride in the front with him. It was the only proper way, he said, to treat foreign guests.

The cab was a standard truck size, a squeeze for three people. Four would have been torture. I asked Mark to explain to Ali that I suffered from claustrophobia and would rather ride in the back.

"He says you'll freeze to death and die," Mark replied.

But I was confident in the powers of my sleeping bag. Riding in the back of the truck would be, I figured, only marginally worse than the bus rides. And considerably less crowded.

This last hope was brought into doubt when Kim and Muhammad said they wanted to go with us. Ali scowled, and told them he would pick them up when he returned from Kashgar. Kim and Muhammad pouted. They wanted to go. It was no problem, they argued; they could ride in the back with me.

Yes! Ali suddenly shouted, they could go, too. He jumped up and down and slapped his brother and friend on the back.

Mark took me aside.

"Do you really think this is a good idea?"

"Yes," I told him, unable to imagine why he would want to ride *any* bus again.

"But we don't know anything about these guys. We don't even know if they can get gas?"

That was a consideration. We'd learned that it took more than money to obtain gas at the infrequent stations. Special gas coupons were required, yet another method of movement control by the government.

Mark asked Ali about fuel. He laughed and thrust out his thumb in a triumphant gesture I remembered from British war movies.

"Do you think that is a yes?" Mark asked.

"You know who these guys remind me of?" Fran said.

"Who?"

"The Monkees. Ali is a dead ringer for Davey Jones."

Ali drove the truck around the corner behind the inn wall. In this hidden spot, they unwrapped a canvas tarpaulin and spread it on the floor of the truck, brushing aside a few hunks of raw, frozen meat. Ali motioned for me to lie on the canvas, and once I was in position, he folded the canvas back over me. Suddenly I was enclosed in a canvas coffin.

"Ali says you'll be warm this way," Mark told me.

It was totally dark under the rough canvas. A moment later, I felt the canvas lift a bit and Ali and Kim climbed under, giggling. They snuggled next to me.

"Hello," Kim said, "what is your name?"

We'd already had this exchange several times but I went along with it and pronounced my name slowly. He repeated it in a serious voice then said, "America, yes?"

It was 800 kilometers to Kashgar. I wondered how long it would take to drive there.

"Ali says to stay out of sight if we stop, okay?" Mark yelled.

"Out of sight?"

We rumbled off toward Kashgar.

I'm not quite sure if under different circumstances, riding through the desert in the back of a dump truck wrapped in a canvas shroud would be so enjoyable. But after the bus, after the bickering with the Public Security Bureaus, the constant chorus of "Meo," it was a great joy to have escaped for a little while the numbing repression and control of modern China. It was a small but sweet victory.

"You name?" Kim asked.

Asku was 200 kilometers away. We left the inn around nine o'clock and I figured we would be on the road two or three hours to Aksu.

It took more than four hours and it seemed longer. Kim and Muhammad agreed it was slow going. Every time the truck slowed a bit, one of them would raise up and yell, "Aksu! Aksu!" Then, when the truck moved on, they would scowl, shaking their heads disapprovingly.

Somehow I drifted to sleep; a fierce pounding on the canvas woke me up. The truck had stopped. Bolting upward, held down by the sleeping bag, I tried to remember where I was.

"Aksu! Aksu!"

This time Kim and Muhammad were right. We scrambled out into the cold desert air.

Ali had stopped in front of a mud hut with a glowing stove out front. Across the street there were more mud huts without lights. The stars were brilliant in the clear night.

Ali walked inside and returned shaking his head. "Ark! Ark!" he shouted.

"What's he saying?" I asked Mark.

"My name," Mark answered. "He has a problem with the m."

"Ark! Ark!"

His brother and Kim took up the cry. They sounded like a bunch of seals circling the truck.

We remounted and drove a few hundred yards to another lighted stand. It was run by a Uighur family; the father was out front cooking, the mother inside making noodles with the help of the children. One of the children was crippled and hobbled around on a crutch.

Inside the stand, it was dark and smoky, lit by a single bulb and a flaring torch in the corner. We sat around a long table. Ali and Muhammad knew the family and they joked back and forth in Uighur.

Ali nodded toward the children. "It is very sad," he whispered, "they do not go to school. All they do is work, even now at two o'clock in the morning."

"But, they make good money," his brother pointed out. "These people look poor but they are not."

"Uighurs know what is important in life!" Ali cried, slapping Mark on the back. "We have a good time, not like the Hans."

Ali shook his finger mockingly at Kim.

"You know what Hans used to do in Korla?" Ali asked us.

We didn't.

"They used to send a Han official to our parties to make certain we didn't dance disco! Have you ever heard of anything so stupid in all your life! They say it is because disco is Western and corrupt but really we think it is because Hans cannot dance. It's true! Kim is a terrible dancer! I am wonderful!"

The young crippled girl brought us plates of dark noodles and lamb with red peppers. Unmarked liters of beer were placed in the center of the table.

"We would all have to come feast with my family in Korla," Ali declared. "We celebrate Ark as the next President of the United States!"

President?

"They think I look like an actor," Mark explained. "And since Reagan is an actor and an American they figure I should be President too."

I remember thinking that there was something disturbing about the amount of sense that made.

"And once I'm President I can get them visas to come to America and live."

"The Chinese are so stupid!" Ali exclaimed, banging his fist on the table. "They tell us we can't travel so of course we want to travel! Everybody should be free to go anywhere they want!"

"Tell us," Muhammad asked, "do you have prostitutes in America?"

As we climbed back in the truck, Ali slapped Mark on the shoulder and said, "Ark! Ark! Shall drive!"

Mark laughed and slid behind the wheel. Ali squeezed beside Fran and punched one of his cassettes into the player. Gerry and the Pacemakers' "Ferry Cross the Mersey" floated over the desert.

I crawled under the canvas, and slid into my sleeping bag.

Ali and Muhammad joined me.

"Your name? Say, please?"

We drove all night. I fell asleep in the canvas cocoon and woke up to hear Mark and Ali talking, the engine dead.

"What's going on?" I yelled.

"Gas stop," Mark said.

Crawling out, I saw we were surrounded by looming sand dunes.

Ali was bent over, sucking on a rubber hose. He jerked it out of his mouth and into the open end of a metal drum in the back of the truck.

Kim and Muhammad stood beside the drum, both smoking. Fran eased them away.

I pulled the canvas back over me and fell asleep.

A long time later, I heard the horn shriek and woke in a panic. Next to me, Kim and Muhammad were grinning. "Kashi! Kashi!" Muhammad yelled.

We threw the covers back and in the distance we could see the glimmer of lights. Ali jumped up and down in the road hugging Fran. Mark sat behind the wheel.

"Kashi!" Ali shouted. "Kashi!"

Chapter
Twenty-Three

Ali stopped beside the gates of a hotel on the outskirts of Kashgar. Suddenly, he appeared nervous,
glancing up and down the road, hustling us off the truck.
We paid our six hundred kuai, and, after a quick hand-
shake, the mad trio climbed back in the truck and sped
away.

We stood by the road slightly dazed. It was mid-
morning, but the sun had not penetrated the fog that
hung over the town. Like refugees, we gathered our be-
longings and walked to the Kashgar Guest House.

It was a big hotel composed of several buildings. All
the doors were locked, and it seemed abandoned. But we
found a Uighur watchman sleeping in the gate house and
woke him up.

He insisted the hotel was open and made a hurried
phone call. A young woman in a purple shawl appeared
twenty minutes later. It was clear she had just woken up.
By our watches it was 10:30.

Yes, she acknowledged, the hotel was open. But we
didn't want to stay there.

Why not?

There hasn't been water for days, she said. Most
of the guests had left. It was terrible. No water, no
food . . .

She shook her head, yawning.

Mark apologized for waking her up and then, pausing for a moment, asked what time it was.

Six-thirty, she replied.

But our watches all read 10:30.

Yes, it was 10:30 too. In Kashgar, she explained, there was Beijing time—that was official time—and Xinjiang time. Most people set their watches to Xinjiang time, four hours earlier than Beijing time.

There was a large clock over the hotel door. It read 10:30.

Oh, yes, she said, all the public clocks are required to be set to official time. But everyone ignores them.

We nodded, then Mark asked if there was another hotel in Kashgar.

She offered to call one for us.

This took a while. But finally she reached the manager of the other hotel on the phone.

He is very full but will make room, she told us. He promises to send his personal car right away for distinguished foreign guests.

We thanked her effusively.

An hour and a half and two phone calls later, an ancient panel truck arrived at the hotel gates. We crawled in the back with a load of cabbages and rode to the city center.

Kashgar seemed to thrive on violence. Ambulances raced the streets in a reckless style guaranteed to produce victims needing their services. Every street had a dentist with a hideous painting of a bloody mouth, usually shown in a vivisected cross view of teeth and gums, over his door. All the Muslim men carried short swords or daggers in their belts. Armed Han troops guarded the intersections and patrolled the back streets.

On the way to the hotel we passed a huge crowd gathered around an overturned truck. Everyone was in very good spirits. We couldn't see what had happened but we heard about it that night on television.

The news announcer introduced the report with a rueful smile. "Some people do not pay enough attention to traffic safety," she lectured. "Here is a good example of what happens to such people." The camera cut to the truck wreck. A bicycle was crumpled underneath the front wheel of the truck. A body, presumably the bicyclist's, lay nearby. There was something odd about the body but it was unclear exactly what until the camera moved closer. The bicyclist had been decapitated. For a long time the camera held a close-up of the torso, still dripping blood. Then in a slow deliberate pan, it moved a few feet across the street to find the severed head. This filled the screen. A policeman nudged it with his foot.

"The city is, not without reason, very prone to spy-fever," Fleming wrote, "and the night we arrived the bizarre rumor ran that a British agent had ridden in from Khotan, accompanied by a White Russian disguised as a woman. This was hard on Kini . . ."

No one, it seems, thought we were spies. But we became suspects in a hotel burglary.

Our hotel had once been the Russian consulate. On the gateposts there was a sign in English that read: JOINT BUILDING-HOTEL WITH CIVILIZATION.

It was not a large building in the normal Russian style but rather a collection of small two-story structures on a dirt street sprinkled with snow. In front of the hotel office rose a grandiose sculpture of a camel ridden by a Uighur. Both the camel and Uighur were scaled to heroic proportions, in the best socialist style, with bulging muscles and determined, strong-jawed faces gazing into the collective future.

The hotel office was lined with wall banners in Chinese. SERVICE IS FERVENT, WAITING ON YOU IS SATISFYING, and TO THE GUESTS THAT ARRIVE, IT IS LIKE COMING HOME read the largest. Our first morning in town, we were summoned to the office by a group of nervous hotel service attendants.

When we arrived at the office, the group of women who normally worked behind the front desk were all in tears. The Han manager looked grim. He was flanked by a pair of well-dressed thugs from the Public Security Bureau.

While the manager looked on apologetically, one of the Public Security officers laid our passports out on the counter. He dealt them crisply, like blackjack cards.

Were these our passports?

It was a silly question. We were the only Westerners staying in the hotel, and we had left our passports the day before at the front desk, as requested.

Yes, we said.

This admission was met with serious glances all around.

When had we arrived in Kashgar?

The day before.

And when were we leaving?

In a few days. We wanted to fly out but had not made reservations.

The Uighur girls cried vigorously in the background.

With more studied glances, we were dismissed.

The next day at the Western Coffee Shop we discovered why we had been questioned. The coffee shop was a wonderful place run by a young Uighur woman enchanted with all things Western. She wore a beret and spoke a little English. The shop was decorated with a jumble of Western cultural artifacts—empty Melitta coffee filter boxes, a L'Eggs panty hose container, a Jack Daniel's bottle filled (much to our disappointment) with water. The Beatles' "Sergeant Pepper's Lonely Hearts Club Band" played continuously.

She was thrilled when we arrived.

"Americans?" she asked hopefully, and when we nodded she blushed and said, "Oh, you must forgive me. I am very sorry. Today my boss is here, and he makes me very nervous." She motioned to the corner where a huge Cossack smiled joylessly, revealing a row of steel teeth. "I am a little nervous and," she giggled, "a little *dronk.*"

She insisted we order Kashgar Burgers, lamb patties served on a bagel-type bread with onions. Maria, as she introduced herself, cooked them on the only electric stove I'd seen in China.

"Oh, I am very sorry that I cook. My partner"—that was her word—"is in Hong Kong to become better Western cook." Then, she started apologizing for the way we had been treated by the Public Security Bureau.

"They were here, asking questions about you," she told us.

"But we've never been here before."

"That is what I told them but I do not think they believed me. Because this is Western Coffee Shop, they think you come here."

Maria told us not to worry about the Public Security; they didn't really think we had stolen anything but it was easier to have foreigners as suspects. "In New China there is no crime," she said, laughing.

I thought about this the next day when Mark and I stumbled across a poster announcing the verdicts of the XINJIANG UIGHUR AUTONOMOUS REGION PEO-

PLE'S MIDDLE SECTION COURT. "These are names," the poster read, "of people who have killed other people and have been killed." There were eleven photographs captioned with names and ages. The black and white photos were covered with a red X. All were Uighur.

The poster was mounted behind a stall selling herbal medicines, run by an old Muslim man who offered dried snakes, toads, a stuffed owl, and various powders, including a locally grown marijuana called Xinjiang tobacco. He spoke no Mandarin, and his explanations of what ailments the various treatments would cure were difficult to comprehend, with one exception. The dried sea horses, he demonstrated graphically, were aphrodisiacs of the finest sort.

The medicine stand was on the edge of the Kashgar bazaar, and it did not seem coincidental that the posters of executed men appeared in this section of town. The bazaar's crowded warren of shops and stalls was indisputably Muslim and Uighur; here in the heart of Kashgar the Communist Hans were foreigners. Stories of knifings and gang fights between Han and Uighur youths made up much of the town's daily conversation.

The Gods have conspired to make Kashgar a troubled place. It stands at the crossroads of different cultures—India and Pakistan to the south, Afghanistan to the west, Russia to the north, and China to the east. At the turn of the century, Kashgar was the centerpiece of what was known as The Great Game, a name the British, with their tendency to confuse war and sport, particularly in those pre-Somme days, gave to the hegemonic maneuverings in Central Asia between England, Russia, Japan, and Germany.

When Fleming crossed China in 1935, the game was intensely underway. He describes seeing a:

. . . striking anti-imperialist poster on the wall of a shrine. It was mainly directed against Japan, who was shown as a fat and oafish fisherman on the point of transfering a fish (Mongolia) from his hook to a basket already containing the flaccid form of Manchukuo; but there was another picture in which Sinkiang, Chinghai, and Lasha were threatened from the west by a lion (representing the Communist armies from Szechwan) and from the east by a tiger which, I learned to my shame, personified Great Britian.

Today the future of China is captured with terrible clarity in the confused streets of Kashgar. Enough of the old town survives to offer a teasing view of mosques and Uighur markets, but the new Kashgar—a relentless monotony of housing blocks and concrete offices—is washing away the Muslim features of this Asian outpost. Soon Kashgar will resemble Xi'an or Beijing.

We made elaborate plans to eat Christmas dinner at the Western Coffee Shop. At Maria's urging, we planned to cook a spectacular feast in her kitchen. "I learn more about cooking your food, and we have a dinner for Jesus birthday," Maria proposed. We spent hours debating menu possibilities.

But on Christmas Day there was no electricity in Maria's restaurant. Since she had an electric stove (her pride and joy), our culinary hopes were dashed. Instead of cooking we sat in the coffee shop, lit by candles, and drank bottle after bottle of Five Star beer. Fran explained to Maria that the candles stuck in old beer bottles would lend a perfect Greenwich Village touch to her coffee shop. This required explaining about Greenwich Village, but it gave us something to do.

Later, stumbling into the street after too many beers and not enough food, I watched a patrol of Han soldiers goose-step down the dirt street. All at once it hit me:

China was like an army—ugly and inefficient, joyless and numbingly monotonous, with little use for art or literature. Like army posts, the towns all looked alike, disposable citadels of crude function, graceless and hateful. It was a country of uniforms, of Cleaning Brigades and Towel Captains.

Back at the hotel, my favorite hall attendant asked me to take a picture of her with a girlfriend. She was about twenty-two and wore a felt leopard-skin box hat with two little orange balls hanging from the brim. Her high-heeled boots were decorated with bits of colored glass glued on in swirling patterns. The two posed hands on hip, perfect Uighur vamps. They flirted with me, coaxing more Polaroids. I used all my film and fell asleep, grinning, while two donkeys brayed incessantly outside the window.

When Fleming and Maillart were in Kashgar they stayed at the British consulate, "a pleasant house with a lovely garden, standing on a little bluff outside the city. . . . we stayed a fortnight in Kashgar, leading a country-house life . . ."

Our accommodations at the JOINT BUILDING-HOTEL WITH CIVILIZATION were definitely less grand, probably the only time on the journey when we could look back enviously at the comfort Maillart and Fleming had enjoyed. But, like our predecessors, "we idled shamelessly in Kashgar, eating and sleeping . . ."

The latter—sleeping—was easier, or at least more enjoyable, than the former. With the Western Coffee Shop out of commission, we concentrated on a noodle stand run by a hustling young Uighur; he was transfixed by Fran and very eager to please. He wore a large white button with #4 on it in red letters; we never could understand why, except like the L'Eggs panty hose containers in the Western Coffee Shop, the button was Western, therefore cool. Behind Fran's back, he would roll his eyes wildly and pound his head with sweeping left hooks.

For purposes of variety, we asked the young Uighur chef if it might be possible for us to have some eggs. He clearly thought this strange but seeing it was something Fran would like, he dispatched an even younger assistant to search for eggs. When the aide returned ten minutes later empty-handed, he was bashed around the head by his boss and sent back out. The blows were delivered with great energy but little force—his boss using his felt cap as the weapon—while everyone packed into the little stand cheered wildly.

Somewhere the assistant found eggs and returned breathless but proud. On his oil drum stove, the cook cracked the eggs into a wok filled with ten inches of bubbling grease and scrambled them. The result was sort of an egg and grease soup, with bits of lamb fat and charred noodles floating with the half-scrambled, half-fried eggs.

Fran took the bowl, smiled, and politely handed it to me. We sat on an old mattress in the corner of the mud room. Nodding at my audience, I lifted a bite with my chopsticks and steered it into my mouth, warm grease dripping over my chin.

I liked it.

After I finished, Fran demonstrated to the chef that it was possible to cook eggs in a good bit less grease. He and all the onlookers were appalled. They clearly thought the end result—nicely scrambled eggs not floating in grease—looked disgusting.

But every day when we returned, the chef knew what we wanted and even stocked a few eggs. To further impress Fran he began opening beer bottles with his teeth and decorated his little stand with a bunch of plastic flowers stuck in a Russian paint can. This all added a nice, homey touch to life in Kashgar.

Chapter
Twenty-Four

"If I was to trust the books I had glanced at in the library at the Consultate-General," Ella Maillart wrote, "there were many for whom Kashgar was a lost city, isolated behind its mountains. For us, on the contrary, Kashgar really represented our true return to civilization, the forty days that lay between us and Srinagar [India] being no more than a final stage."

Like Fleming and Maillart, Kashgar was a symbolic, but not actual, end to our travels. Their final destination was India; ours was Beijing.

By all rights, returning to Beijing should have been a snap.

"We can fly back," I assured Mark and Fran. "There's an airport in Kashgar. With regular flights. There's nothing to it."

That, of course, turned out to be wrong.

In theory, the purchase of a ticket on CAAC, the Chinese airline, was simple. There was an office. You went there and gave them money. They gave you a ticket.

But it didn't work out that way. We discovered this when we arrived at the CAAC office, a concrete bunker on a wide street near the bazaar. Mark and I followed a group of Hans through the blanket over the doorway.

When our turn came at the counter, we faced a squat Han with the expressionless features of a man used to dealing with a disappointed public. He talked as if reading from a script.

"We would like to buy a ticket to Beijing," Mark said, beaming. He had confided that the closer we got to the Coffee Shop of the Great Wall Sheraton, the happier he felt. We talked about food a lot in Kashgar.

The airline cadre named a price and told us we must pay in FEC. We nodded and brought out money. He nodded and brought out tickets. It was all so easy, I thought I was dreaming.

He handed us the tickets. Overjoyed, Mark and I fondled the crisp paper. Unlike train and bus passes, which were made of colored tissue paper, the plane tickets were big and stiff and even had a picture of a pretty Russian plane flying through a cloudless sky. That the sky was actually a light green color did not bother me.

"There is no date here . . ." Mark noted politely, pointing to the blank space for departure date.

"Yes, there is not."

"But when does the plane leave?"

The official grunted and pointed to a schedule under the glass counter top. It indicated three departures a week.

"So we could go tomorrow?" Mark asked, pointing to the next scheduled flight.

"There is no room."

This was said without examining any documents. It had a ring of natural finality, like "The sun comes up in the East."

Mark asked when the next flight might be with open seats.

This prompted a long diatribe against the weather and its ruthless effect on air travel. Many flights had been cancelled. The waiting list was long.

Though snow covered the ground, the weather since we'd arrived in Kashgar had been clear. It was hard to imagine how it might improve.

"So when do you think we might be able to fly to Beijing?" Mark asked nervously.

"Fly to Beijing?" The official's tone indicated it was a novel idea. "There are no flights to Beijing from Kashgar."

This provoked one of those preposterously dramatic silences while Mark and I gawked at our tickets. It said Beijing, we were sure of it.

"From Kashgar you can fly to Ürümqi—when the weather improves. From there you can talk to the office about a flight to Beijing. If there are any flights, you can use this ticket."

"Isn't there a way we can book a seat all the way through even if we have to change in Ürümqi?"

This ludicrous suggestion seemed to brighten the official's day. He chuckled and said, "Meo."

That evening, while having our regular omelet at the noodle stand, Mark spent a long time staring at the Polaroids of his girlfriend. Later, we drank a bottle of Russian vodka we found in the bazaar. It helped, a little.

During our third day waiting at the airport, the PLA security detail decided to test the metal detector. The procedure began with a large Hami melon removed from a crate labeled XINJIANG TREASURES. The guards placed the melon in the X-ray machine. They observed the results gravely, nodding to each other like consulting surgeons. They then opened the machine and plunged a long, gold-handled dagger—the kind of knife all Muslims in Kashgar carried—into the melon. This was X-rayed. Several more daggers were embedded into the melon and X-rayed.

When the melon finally fell apart, the guards ate it, using the plate of the machine as a table.

After three days waiting for a plane, the Kashgar airport was beginning to feel like home to us. Each morning at seven we loaded our bags into a taxi and rode to the airport. Although we arrived in the dark, there was always a crowd of Chinese already in line at the ticket counter. Each day we stacked our bags in line. Since our status was strictly stand-by, position was critical. A large chalkboard proclaimed that the flight would leave at 11:00. Though written in chalk supposedly for ease of alteration, this departure time was never changed.

Each day we would wait as the lobby filled with expectant passengers. The 11 o'clock departure time came and went. We waited all day. And then, around 7:00 P.M., when no planes had arrived or departed, we returned to the hotel.

By the third day, I had begun to suspect that the airport was in truth a prop for some elaborate deception, no more useful than the plywood docks and destroyers the Allies employed to trick German intelligence about D-day preparations.

The scene certainly had a military feel. Young Han troops drilled on the tarmac from dawn to dusk. These teenagers carried wooden rifles and were the happiest group I'd seen in China. They appeared to revel in the discipline, working hard to please their lean, handsome drill sergeants. In the latrine on the edge of the runway, the only toilet at the airport, the recruits admired each other's uniforms, fingering the thick green wool, the shiny metal buttons. They wore white gloves of a rough cotton, like gardener's gloves, and brown fur hats mounted with a red star.

The airport looked like a bus station, with no visible signs—like radar or control tower—normally associated with the movement of planes. The only sign that it might be a place visited by planes—apparently rarely—was the long stretch of asphalt where the troops drilled. After their afternoon drilling, the troops were issued shovels and they hacked away at the ice lining the edges of the runway.

While we waited, there were no announcements, but, hourly, rumors buzzed around the waiting room, which had begun to look like a refugee camp. The lack of information created some tension between Mark and me. My need to ask questions battled against his inclination to wait. "I think we'll know it if a plane comes," he replied when I badgered him to help me find someone who might know what was happening. On the second day, I met a young official who spoke a little English. He hung out in a back room with his pals, smoking cigarettes and perusing aviation magazines. (I feared this might be their only contact with planes.) They welcomed a new face and, in a tortured way, we discussed the merits of different aircraft. They were very disappointed when I told them that the Concorde was narrow and uncomfortable and made a lot of noise.

Toward the end of the third day, the plane arrived. There was no announcement. The faint throb of the distant engines electrified the crowd. After a stunned pause, there was a mad dash toward the check-in counter. Though I scrambled along with everyone else, I didn't understand the logic of the rush. Since all prospective passengers had placed their luggage in a long line winding from the counter, one's place in line had been already established.

But not so. While some people did take a position next to their luggage, most used this point as a staging ground for valiant assaults toward the front. I felt like I had been caught in a fire-crazed crowd fleeing toward an exit.

The roar of the plane thundered through the building, adding to the panic. Windows shook. I could feel vibrations through the floor, and for a moment I thought the pilot had erred and the plane would crash into the waiting room.

As the plane landed, a semblance of order returned to the line, like a major battle that had subsided with continuing skirmishes on the edges. An official appeared behind the counter. This really is going to happen, I thought. Then, everyone started to drift toward the exits. I had heard no announcement. That sickening feeling of being the last one to know anything—a feeling that had become very familiar—returned.

A few minutes later, we learned what everyone else seemed to know telepathically—the flight would not leave today. It was too late, and the pilot did not like to fly after dark.

We slunk back to the JOINT BUILDING-HOTEL WITH CIVILIZATION.

It was the most wonderful flight of my life. I reclined in the plane in a happy daze, occasionally glancing out the window just to remind myself of the distances we were traveling. No one had spit on my feet or vomited next to me. It was warm. The seat was soft. Then, the plane dipped down out of the clear sky into clouds. We were landing in Ürümqi, just an hour and a half after leaving Kashgar. This was heaven.

And then I heard Fran scream. I looked at her across the aisle. She was staring out the window with a terrified look.

The plane had broken through the cloud cover. We were over a city; something was wrong.

"Oh my God," Fran said. "Those smokestacks—"

"What?"

"They're higher than we are—"

The plane jerked upward, back into the clouds. A little murmur of fearful laughter rolled through the cabin.

"I was looking *up* at the smokestacks," Fran said. "I promise you, I was."

We flew around in the clouds for a long time, circling and occasionally dipping down like a wounded pigeon. Next to me, a woman vomited into the paper bag CAAC had provided. She also appeared to be crying. Her husband looked on disgustedly.

"Did I ever tell you what CAAC stands for?" Mark asked. He was reading Stephen King and appeared quite content.

"No."

"Chinese Airlines Always Crashes."

The plane nosed into a steep dive. We broke through the clouds and plopped down almost instantly onto a runway. Tires screeching, the Russian plane skidded to a stop.

"Thank God," Fran murmured. I felt the same way. We started to get up but were waved down by one of the stewardesses.

We sat on the runway for over an hour. No one complained. No one explained. The stewardesses passed out little plastic packages containing combs and toothbrushes. This smacked of an extended delay of the overnight variety and made me very nervous. I looked at Mark, hoping he would ask one of the stewardesses how long it might be before we could get off, but he was buried behind *Salem's Lot.* Rising to use the bathroom, I was gently pushed back into my seat by a stewardess.

It was all beginning to feel like a polite hijacking. We sat there for another hour. Children urinated on the floor and the smell was appalling. Finally, a particularly impressive-looking cadre-type said something to one of the stewardesses.

"No mistake was made. The weather was just bad," she told him curtly.

It hit me then. We weren't in Ürümqi. We had landed at the wrong town.

This panicked Fran. "You mean we'll have to do all that over again?"

"All what?"

"Take off, land."

"What we've got to do," I told Mark, "is find out how close we are to Ürümqi. If we're not far, let's demand they let us off and we can take a bus the rest of the way."

"You've got to be kidding."

The engines started. The high voice of the stewardess came over the loudspeaker. Mark relaxed.

"We're going to Ürümqi," he said, looking relieved.

"We'll just have to see," I said, pulling out a compass. "I'm not sure I believe them. If we head west back to Kashgar, call the stewardess and demand to go back."

"I think I'm going to kill you."

We quit talking after that, amazed at what we were seeing. Apparently troubled by the overcast, the pilot decided to fly under the clouds all the way to Ürümqi. These clouds were very low. Often, we appeared to be skimming the ground. I looked out the window and realized that we were following a road. I could see drivers in their trucks; some stuck their heads out of the window and gazed up, panic-stricken. Others swerved off into the desert, convinced, understandably, that the plane was going to land, or crash, on the blacktop. The woman beside me opened her mouth wide in a silent scream. She had bad teeth, like broken rocks.

When we landed, no one moved until the stewardesses insisted we were in Ürümqi and the flight was over.

At the plane's door, the head stewardess gave me a little pin of wings emblazoned with CAAC! I wore it like a medal.

Chapter
Twenty-Five

B efore leaving for Kashgar, Beijing struck me as a massive tragedy; one of the great metropolises in history stripped of all grace and joy. But after a couple of months on China's frontiers, Beijing's advantages were vivid.

First, there were restaurants. Yes, they were cold and dirty and they closed at 7:00 P.M. But there were actually more than one or two of them, and some variety of cuisine was available. Our hotel, for example, had three sushi bars. Honest.

I had decided to stay at the Xinqiao Hotel because it was directly across the street from the old British legation. I'd been reading *Siege of Peking* and wanted to explore what had once been the center of European life in Beijing, when there was such a thing, and how it had changed.

The Xinqiao had been a cadre school during the Cultural Revolution. After Nixon re-opened China, it became a hotel again and enjoyed a spate of popularity with Americans. Its ballroom-sized restaurant was touted as offering the best Western food in Beijing. The chocolate sundaes were legendary among foreign correspondents. Now the Americans had moved to posher quarters like the Great Wall Sheraton, and scores of Japanese businessmen have taken over. Sushi has replaced sundaes.

The ultimate goal of the Four Modernizations, Deng Xiaoping has announced, is to put China on a technological level with Japan by the year 2000. This seems an admirable though ambitious notion for a country that did not have a functioning university barely a decade ago; a country that in the Cultural Revolution lost an entire generation to peasant worship. But there is money to be made in the effort, and the offices of Japanese companies line the halls of the Xinqiao Hotel. Some are famous —Hitachi, Control Data, Suzuki; others obscure but seemingly profitable—Tanyo Fisheries, Onika Construction, Kopmatosa Forklifts.

What startled me most about the Japanese businessmen was their style of dress. Almost to a man (and they are all men), they wore the clothes of English country gentlemen, all tweeds and sweaters. Many smoked pipes. Ralph Lauren was very popular. It was not uncommon to turn a corner and come across a group of Japanese men who appeared to have just returned from pheasant hunting on their estate. Some even wore knee-high riding boots.

"We are like soldiers," one Japanese businessman told me when I asked if he liked working in Beijing. "We go where we are sent and do what we are told." Even with the sushi bars of the Xinqiao, Beijing must be a tough assignment. Away from their families, forced to live in small apartments, engaged in daily struggles with the Chinese bureaucracy, their's is not an easy life. Like soldiers everywhere, the Japanese businessmen look to drink to ease their plight. Lots of drink.

But even staggering down the halls, arm in arm, the businessmen maintain their legendary politeness. One evening I was standing at the attendant's hall desk trying to explain that the lock on my closet door was jammed. As all my clothes were in the closet, this was a problem. I was dressed in multi-colored paisley underwear and a bright orange sweater. I was also wearing boots.

Two Japanese gentlemen stopped and offered to help.

They wore Harris tweed jackets, rep ties, and gray slacks. Both were very drunk.

"May we please be of assistance?"

I explained the problem. They started speaking in Chinese. The attendant, a kindly older man with a perfectly bald head and a drooping mustache, responded.

"He says there is no key," one of the Japanese explained. "But he will knock the lock out." The attendant brandished a large hammer and what looked like a railroad spike. I wondered if this was standard issue to all attendants.

"What happened to the key?" I asked. "There must be one somewhere."

"He says it was lost in the Cultural Revolution."

"Oh."

The attendant said something that the Japanese translated.

"There is a charge, of course, for this service."

"But . . ."

"It is only five quai." Both Japanese were grinning. So was I.

"Personally," the Japanese said, suddenly looking very serious, "I think it is worth five quai just to see this. My friend and I will be glad to contribute if you allow us the pleasure of watching."

On New Year's Eve I sat at my window and watched snow fall on Beijing while listening to the news stations of the West on my short-wave radio. The Voice of America, Radio Sweden, Radio Switzerland—all led with stories of China in turmoil. They made it sound as if Beijing was the scene of an ongoing pitched battle between students and police.

But in Beijing it was difficult to find anyone who would admit that even one demonstration had occurred. Direct questions—"What do you think about the demonstrators?"—were met with shrugs and nervous giggles.

Then I met a foreign correspondent who claimed to know all the inner machinations of the student leaders. "This afternoon, 3 o'clock, at Tiananmen square. A demo is going to happen," he would tell me. So I'd walk the mile or so from the Xinqiao and wait in the massive square, flanked by the Great Hall of the People and Chairman Mao Memorial Hall. The scale of such places is designed, of course, to reinforce the insignificance of the individual, and Tiananmen square accomplishes this admirably. In the snow and ripping wind, I would strain to see across the huge space, hoping to spot a demonstration. Several times I thought I saw trouble developing and ran quickly to the spot only to find teenage students on a field trip or a rowdy tour of Hong Kong Chinese. Once I was unsure and asked, "Is this a demonstration?" They answered politely, "No, it is not. But we like very much to practice our English. Will you help?"

After several trips to the square based on sure-fire tips, I began to think everyone was right: the demonstrations were a creation of the Western news media.

But just like the compulsive gambler who bets on every tip but the good ones, I wasn't around when the real demonstration did occur. It was New Year's Day about 6:00 A.M. My friend, the correspondent, had called the night before touting, as usual, the latest rumor. But when he said we needed to be on the square at 4:30, I laughed out loud. At least he was paid to endure this sort of insanity. I was just curious.

But had I been there at 4:30 I would have seen a very interesting sight: the police ingeniously flooded the square with fire hoses. When the demonstrators massed and attempted to move toward the Great Hall of the People, they skidded around like tops. A few were arrested. Everyone went home.

Peter Fleming died in 1971, a victim of a heart attack while grouse hunting. "His life had been extinguished suddenly, without pain, after a moment of intense satisfaction in pursuit of the sport he loved best," Duff Hart-Davis, his biographer, wrote.

Ella Maillart, however, still lived in Geneva. I'd called her before leaving America, and she sounded like a feisty woman with little time for reminiscence. But I wanted to meet her.

The question was: how should I get to Geneva? The only proper way to do it was obvious—take the Trans-Siberian railway back to Europe. To be honest, I was in no hurry to get back on a plane.

Against the backdrop of demonstrations, Fran and I made daily trips to the various embassies, trying to obtain the visas necessary for the Trans-Siberian. This game quickly came to resemble a college scavenger hunt.

We had to get papers from the Russian, Mongolian, and Polish embassies, plus deal with CITS to book space on the train. The list read like an International Who's Who of Nightmare Bureaucracies, the true royalty of confusion. The embassies each had bizarre and conflicting opening hours—the Mongolian, I think, was open two hours a week on different days each month—and each visa had to be obtained in a specific order. The Russians wouldn't talk to you unless you had a Mongolian stamp, and the Poles insisted you have Russian clearance first, although they might make exceptions. . . . And of course the Chinese wouldn't consider booking a seat for you unless you had *all* the papers while the Mongolians didn't want to issue a visa if you didn't have a ticket . . .

All of this madness was carried on in sub-zero weather amid intermittent snowstorms. The snow was particularly annoying because Beijing taxi drivers viewed a few flakes of snow with the same seriousness as a saturation bombing attack.

The scavenger-hunt atmosphere was heightened by the recurring cast of characters one encountered each step of the way. There were about ten of us trying to weave our way through this maze. There was a blond Australian law student named Peter, who had become separated from his "mate" and asked each time we ran into him, "You seen Bob around, have you?" As if we might have downed a few pints of lager the night before with Bob and the boys at the pub.

Peter later teamed up with Nigel, an aging punk rocker from London. I thought he was an incredible bore until one day in the lobby of the Polish embassy—one of our second homes—Fran pressed him about his travel experiences and he erupted with the most appalling stories of near-death encounters in the wilds of Nepal and Bhutan.

In the silence that once followed a rendition a near deadly encounter with Tibetan dogs, Nigel asked me, "You don't like living in New York, do you?"

"Well, yes. Why?"

"Isn't it a terribly violent place?"

We also met a pair of young German mountaineers, ardent pacifists, who made the rounds sensibly dressed in bright orange survival gear; and a woman who spoke English with some vague middle-European accent and pretended, for some reason, not to be an American. Later I discovered she was a school teacher from Duluth.

The Trans-Siberian left Beijing at 7:30 A.M. Although we arrived at the station an hour early, the Foreign Guest waiting room was already crowded with Russians. They wore beautiful fur hats and slapped each other on the back while sipping from vodka bottles, just like Russians were supposed to.

Fran and I had put Mark on the plane to New York the day before. The last day or so he had been so happy to be leaving that he had begun to get almost sentimental about our journey.

"It *was* a good trip, wasn't it?" He'd said at our farewell dinner of Beijing duck.

"Mark," Fran reminded him, "you hated it. You hate China, remember?"

"I know, but . . ." He shrugged. A beggar hovering in the background darted in to steal a little duck off our table.

"I am glad I went," he said. "At least, I think I am. I probably am."

We left it at that, but I think he knew we were glad as well.

Waiting for the platform gates to be opened, I took a last walk through the cavernous Beijing station. It was frantic with rushing bodies. A large poster caught my eye.

Under a row of bright red characters were four color photographs taken inside train compartments. Each photo featured the victim of some hideous calamity. In one, a person had been blown into a luggage rack above a seat. His intestines dripped down like a bad effect from a cheap horror film. Another photo showed a close-up of a man missing the lower part of his face.

An appreciative crowd had gathered around the poster. There were many giggles.

The two German mountaineers passed by carrying massive packs. One, I knew, read Chinese.

"What does this say?" I asked.

"A Tale of Blood," he pronounced in a thick accent. "This is what happens to people who carry fireworks on trains."

Fran came running out of the waiting room. "They're loading," she announced, stopping to stare at the poster.

"I'm going to miss this country," she said after a moment. "I really am."

We hurried back to the waiting room, dragged our bags and skis past the Russians—now crying and hugging each other—and climbed onto the train.

Just as the conductors were shutting the doors, Peter the Australian ran onto the platform trailed by two Chinese. All three carried huge cardboard boxes.

He passed the boxes up to us, embraced his porters and scrambled aboard, panting. The train started to move.

"What's this?" I asked, still holding a heavy box.

"Beer," he said. "Just last night I heard this terrible rumor that Gorbachev had banned all liquor on trains. Can you imagine? Eight days." He shook his head, horrified.

"How much?"

"A case a day. It was all I could carry. But with proper rationing it should see us through. What do you say to a little Five Star for breakfast? A nice way to leave China, huh?"

We said it sounded wonderful.

Acknowledgments

This book would not have been written without Carl Navarre and Don Cutler, and it wouldn't have been any fun without Marjorie Braman.

Zack and Julie Goodyear set the right tone from the start and did more than they know to keep it that way. Len Krassner solved midnight emergencies and Harry McKeon and Charlie Donadio consistently improved my outlook on life.

Karen Frishman of Patagonia, Inc. and Kim Vanderhaven of Jansport provided unflappable technical support, helping thwart the prediction, "You will freeze to death and die."

A special thanks to the Stuart Irbys for letting me hide out at their wonderful place for the final stages.

And, of course, none of this would have been possible without Mark, David, and Fran.

About the Author

Stuart Stevens grew up in Jackson, Mississippi. As a political consultant, he has directed media campaigns in numerous Senate, Congressional, and gubernatorial contests. In 1984 he became the first person to race the complete Worldloppet International ski circuit in one year, a story told in the television documentary "Marathon Winter." His articles and stories have appeared in *The New Republic, Washington Monthly, Skiing, Esquire, International Herald Tribune,* and *Washingtonian,* among others. He is currently writing a book for the Atlantic Monthly Press about a trans-Saharan journey.